EXECUTIVE SUMMARY

This White Paper is written by Commodity Futures Trading Commission (CFTC or Commission) Commissioner J. Christopher Giancarlo, a public supporter of the swaps market reforms passed by Congress in Title VII of the Dodd-Frank Act, namely clearing swaps through central counterparties, reporting swaps to trade repositories and executing swaps transactions on regulated trading platforms. The author supports the CFTC's implementation of the first two reforms, but is critical of the CFTC's implementation of the third, as explained in this White Paper.

This paper (a) analyzes flaws in the CFTC's implementation of its swaps trading regulatory framework under Title VII of the Dodd-Frank Act and (b) proposes a more effective alternative.

This paper begins with a broad overview of the complex structure of the global swaps market. It then reviews the clear legislative provisions of Title VII of the Dodd-Frank Act. Next, it reviews in detail the Commission's flawed implementation of the Dodd-Frank Act's swaps trading provisions.

This paper asserts that there is a fundamental mismatch between the CFTC's swaps trading regulatory framework and the distinct liquidity and trading dynamics of the global swaps market. It explains that the Commission's framework is highly over-engineered, disproportionately modeled on the U.S. futures market and biased against both human discretion and technological innovation. As such, the CFTC's framework does not accord with the letter or spirit of the Dodd-Frank Act.

This paper identifies the following adverse consequences of the flawed swaps trading rules:

- Driving global market participants away from transacting with entities subject to CFTC swaps regulation.

- Fragmenting swaps trading into numerous artificial market segments.

- Increasing market liquidity risk.

- Making it highly expensive and burdensome to operate SEFs.

- Hindering swaps market technological innovation.

- Opening the U.S. swaps market to algorithmic and high-frequency trading.

- Wasting taxpayer money when the CFTC is seeking additional resources.

- Jeopardizing relations with foreign regulators.

- Threatening U.S. job creation and human discretion in swaps execution.

- Increasing market fragility and the systemic risk that the Dodd-Frank regulatory reform was predicating on reducing.

This White Paper proposes an alternative swaps trading framework that is pro-reform. It offers a comprehensive, cohesive and flexible alternative that better aligns with swaps market dynamics and is more true to congressional intent. The framework is built upon five clear tenets:

- **Comprehensiveness:** Subject the broadest range of U.S. swaps trading activity to CFTC oversight.

- **Cohesiveness:** Remove artificial segmentation of swaps trading and regulate all CFTC swaps trading in a holistic fashion.

- **Flexibility:** Return to the Dodd-Frank Act's express prescription for flexibility in swaps trading by permitting trade execution through "any means of interstate commerce," allowing organic development of swaps products and market structure, accommodating beneficial swaps market practices and respecting the general nature of core principles.

- **Professionalism:** Raise standards of professionalism in the swaps market by establishing requirements for product and market knowledge, professionalism and ethical behavior for swaps market personnel.

- **Transparency:** Increase transparency through a balanced focus on promoting swaps trading and market liquidity as Congress intended.

This White Paper asserts that its pro-reform agenda would yield a broad range of benefits. It would:

- Align with congressional intent to promote swaps trading under CFTC regulation.

- Promote vibrant swaps markets by regulating swaps trading in a manner well matched to underlying market dynamics.

- Reduce global and domestic fragmentation in the swaps market.

- Foster market liquidity.

- Reduce burdensome legal and compliance costs of registering and operating CFTC-registered SEFs.

- Encourage technological innovation to better serve market participants and preserve jobs of U.S.-based support personnel.

- Free up CFTC resources and save taxpayer money at a time of large federal budget deficits.

- Provide another opportunity for the CFTC to coordinate with other jurisdictions that are implementing their own swaps trading rules.

- Reverse the increasing fragility of the U.S. swaps market by allowing organic development and growth for greater U.S. economic health and prosperity.

Of Note:

1. Commissioner Giancarlo asserts that the CFTC's swaps trading rules do not accord with Title VII of the Dodd-Frank Act. He calls for greater adherence to the express language of Title VII in conformance with congressional intent.

2. Commissioner Giancarlo contends that the CFTC's swaps trading rules increase rather than decrease the systemic risk that the Dodd-Frank Act was premised on reducing.

3. Commissioner Giancarlo contends that the CFTC's restrictive and over-engineered swaps trading rules have failed to achieve their ostensible objective of meaningful pre-trade price transparency.

4. Commissioner Giancarlo contends that the CFTC's swaps trading rules add unprecedented regulatory complexity without meaningful benefit wasting taxpayer money at a time when the CFTC is seeking additional funding.

5. Commissioner Giancarlo contends that the CFTC's rules open the U.S. swaps market to algorithmic and high-frequency trading that is not otherwise present.

6. Commissioner Giancarlo is the first CFTC Commissioner to call for and put forth a proposal to raise the standards of professional conduct for swaps market personnel.

7. Commissioner Giancarlo proposes a comprehensive, cohesive and transparent swaps trading framework that is pro-reform and better aligns with swaps market dynamics and the express provisions of Title VII of the Dodd-Frank Act.

TABLE OF CONTENTS

INTRODUCTION: Why a White Paper?

> What is at stake in our economic decisions today is not some grand
> warfare of rival ideologies which will sweep the country with passion but
> the practical management of a modern economy. What we need is not
> labels and clichés but more basic discussion of the sophisticated and
> technical questions involved in keeping a great economic machinery
> moving ahead.

John F. Kennedy[1]

In September 2008, Lehman Brothers filed for Chapter 11 bankruptcy protection. Its failure was a consequence of the bursting of a double bubble of housing prices and consumer credit as lenders became concerned about a fall in property values and the repayment of mortgages. Lehman's demise came amidst a global "run on the bank," in which rapidly falling asset values looked to prevent U.S. and foreign lenders from meeting their cash obligations. This event marked the beginning of a full-blown financial crisis that was devastating for too many American businesses and families.

Bilaterally executed over-the-counter (OTC) swaps amplified and spread the financial crisis. Some counterparties who entered into such swaps had inadequately collateralized exposures that caused swaps users to face huge losses as counterparty defaults appeared likely. Because there was little public information about bilateral exposures among swaps users, third parties were less willing to provide credit to institutions that possibly faced such losses. Fear for the stability of the global banking system led the U.S. government to inject emergency capital into the largest U.S. banks and insurance companies at great expense to American taxpayers.

I remember the 2008 financial crisis very well. I served for over thirteen years as a senior executive of a U.S. wholesale brokerage firm that operates global trading platforms for bank-to-bank swaps transactions. I remember the panic in the eyes of bank executives and the tremor in the voices of bank regulators. I saw how fear drove

---

[1] John F. Kennedy, XXXV President of the United States: 1961-1963, *234 - Commencement Address at Yale University* (Jun. 11, 1962), *available at* http://www.presidency.ucsb.edu/ws/?pid=29661.

the crisis: fear of counterparty failure among the major swaps dealing banks and fear among regulators of their lack of visibility into counterparty credit exposure.

The experience confirmed my unwavering support for greater transparency into counterparty credit risk and trading data and increased central counterparty (CCP) clearing of swaps.[2] Although not driven by the crisis,[3] I also support sensible regulation of swaps trading and execution to raise trading standards and bring swaps markets more in line with the standards of conduct in other capital markets, such as equities and futures.

Upon passage of the Dodd-Frank Wall Street Reform and Consumer Protection Act (Dodd-Frank Act)[4] in July 2010, I publicly commended the work of the President and Congress to enhance the safety and soundness of the OTC derivatives markets.[5] Since that time, I have been a consistent advocate for practical and effective implementation of the following three pillars of Title VII of the Dodd-Frank Act:[6] reporting swaps data to trade repositories, executing swaps on regulated trading platforms and clearing swaps

---

[2] Even before the 2008 financial crisis, I was involved in an independent effort by non-Wall Street banks to develop a central clearing house for credit default swaps. *See, e.g.,* GFI Group Inc., *GFI Group Inc. and ICAP plc To Acquire Ownership Stakes In The Clearing Corporation,* PRNewswire, Dec. 21, 2006, *available at* http://www.prnewswire.com/news-releases/gfi-group-inc-and-icap-plc-to-acquire-ownership-stakes-in-the-clearing-corporation-57223742.html. *See also Testimony Before the H. Committee on Financial Services on Implementation of the Dodd-Frank Wall Street Reform and Consumer Protection Act,* 112th Cong. 8 (2011) (statement of J. Christopher Giancarlo) ("In 2005, GFI Group and ICAP Plc, a wholesale broker and fellow member of the WMBAA, took minority stakes in the Clearing Corp and worked together to develop a clearing facility for credit default swaps. That initiative ultimately led to greater dealer participation and the sale of the Clearing Corp to the Intercontinental Exchange and the creation of ICE Trust, a leading clearer of credit derivative products.").

[3] Markets for credit default swaps and other OTC derivatives remained open and well-functioning throughout the 2008 financial crisis. *See* Peter J. Wallison, Bad History, Worse Policy: How a False Narrative about the Financial Crisis Led to the Dodd-Frank Act 535 (AEI Press 2013) (Wallison).

[4] Dodd-Frank Wall Street Reform and Consumer Protection Act, Public Law 111-203, 124 Stat. 1376 (2010).

[5] *Wholesale Markets Brokers' Association, Americas Commends Historic US Financial Legislation, GFI Group Inc.,* Jul. 21, 2010, *available at* http://gfigroup.investorroom.com/index.php?s=43&item=158.

[6] J. Christopher Giancarlo, Commissioner, Keynote Address of CFTC Commissioner J. Christopher Giancarlo at The Global Forum for Derivatives Markets, 35th Annual Burgenstock Conference, Geneva, Switzerland: The Looming Cross-Atlantic Derivatives Trade War: "A Return to Smoot-Hawley" (Sep. 24, 2014), *available at* http://www.cftc.gov/PressRoom/SpeechesTestimony/opagiancarlos-1; *Testimony Before the H. Committee on Financial Services on Implementation of the Dodd-Frank Wall Street Reform and Consumer Protection Act,* 112th Cong. 7-19 (2011) (statement of J. Christopher Giancarlo).

through CCPs.[7] My professional and commercial experience, not academic theory or political ideology, drives my support for these reforms. Simply put, well-regulated markets are good for American business and job creation. That is why I support swaps market reform.

I commend the CFTC for its generally successful implementation of CCP clearing. I also support the CFTC's data reporting mandate, the implementation of which remains a work in progress. I am, however, critical of the CFTC's swaps trading rules. I believe they are fundamentally flawed for reasons set forth in this White Paper, the foremost of which is that the CFTC rules neither enhance trading liquidity nor accord with the express requirements of the Dodd-Frank Act.

There is a fundamental mismatch between the CFTC's swaps trading regulatory framework and the distinct liquidity, trading and market structure characteristics of the global swaps markets. This misalignment was caused by inappropriately applying to global swaps trading a U.S.-centric futures regulatory model that supplants human discretion with overly complex and highly prescriptive rules in contravention of congressional intent. This mismatch – and the application of this framework worldwide – has caused numerous harms, foremost of which is driving global market participants away from transacting with entities subject to CFTC swaps regulation, resulting in fragmented global swaps markets. In addition, the CFTC's rules carve swaps trading into numerous artificial market segments, fragmenting markets domestically. This fragmentation has exacerbated the already inherent challenge in swaps trading – adequate liquidity – and thus is increasing market fragility and the systemic risk that the Dodd-Frank reforms were predicated on reducing.

---

[7] The author readily acknowledges that CCP clearing is not a panacea for counterparty credit risk. CCP clearing does not extinguish risk, but transfers and centralizes it into one or more clearinghouses. *See* Wallison at 419-421. Yet, with proper management of CCP margin requirements, credit reserves operations to uniform standards of best practices and competent regulatory supervision, the benefit of CCP clearing is its potential to attract more counterparties into trading markets, thereby enhancing transactional liquidity and reducing counterparty concentration. Nevertheless, the author is sympathetic to concerns that clearinghouses themselves – now required to clear trillions of dollars in trades – are too big to fail. *See* Wallison at 537.

Vibrant and competitive financial markets must work hand-in-hand with smart and well-designed regulations to support a strong U.S. economy. Flawed and ill-suited swaps market regulation arbitrarily increases the cost of risk management, repels global capital, diminishes trading liquidity and stymies the legitimate use of derivatives causing the economy as a whole to suffer. I have written this White Paper to address these and other concerns.

It is not too late to get these rules right. This paper proposes an alternative regulatory framework that is pro-reform. It is comprehensive in scope and more flexible in application. This alternative focuses on raising standards of professional conduct for swaps market personnel rather than dictating prescriptive and ill-suited trading rules. It provides flexibility so that market participants can choose the manner of trade execution best suited to their swaps trading and liquidity needs. It better aligns regulatory oversight with inherent swaps market dynamics. Crucially, the alternative fully aligns with Title VII of the Dodd-Frank Act to promote swaps trading under CFTC regulation and attract, rather than repel, global capital to U.S. trading markets. The alternative seeks to lessen the market fragility and fragmentation that have arisen as a consequence of the CFTC's flawed swaps trading regime.

This paper is organized as follows: Section I examines global swaps trading that evolved in the decades before the Dodd-Frank Act. Section II reviews Congress's intended swaps trading regulatory framework as set out in Title VII. Section III details the major aspects of the CFTC's faulty swaps trading regulatory framework. Section IV discusses the adverse consequences of this flawed regime. Section V proposes an alternative regulatory framework. Section VI concludes with an appeal for a new and non-partisan effort to reconsider CFTC swaps trading rules to better align them with the inherent nature of swaps trading in global markets and the clear instructions of Title VII of the Dodd-Frank Act.

I believe the current Commission, led by Chairman Massad, has a budding spirit of cooperation and pragmatism. In my first few months at the Commission, I have been impressed with the knowledge, dedication and professionalism of my fellow

Commissioners and the CFTC staff. The Commission and staff carry a long and proud history of smart and principled regulation of the U.S. futures market. I believe they are committed to implementing and operating a similarly successful regulatory framework for the U.S. swaps market. In this regard, criticism herein of the CFTC's swaps trading regulatory framework is not directed at the dedicated CFTC staff, who under the direction of Chairman Massad and the Commissioners, continue to work diligently to apply the CFTC's ill-fitting rule set to the unique characteristics of global swaps markets. Unfortunately, the CFTC staff and particularly staff of the Division of Market Oversight are faced with the Sisyphean task of making swaps trading succeed in an unsuitable futures-style regime.

I wish to thank the members of my professional staff, Marcia Blase, Jason Goggins and Amir Zaidi, for their insightful and substantive contributions.[8] Nevertheless, the views and opinions expressed herein are my own and do not necessarily reflect the views of the CFTC, other CFTC Commissioners or the CFTC staff.

---

[8] I would also like to thank my legal interns, Chelsea Pizzola and Michael Selig from The George Washington University Law School, for their editorial assistance.

I. THE NATURE OF GLOBAL SWAPS TRADING

The use of derivatives to manage commercial or market risk dates back thousands of years.[9] Derivatives allow users to guard against gains or declines in the values of underlying financial assets, such as physical commodities, interest rates, stocks, bonds, trading indices or currencies. They serve this purpose without requiring the user to buy or sell the underlying assets. In this regard, derivatives are akin to risk insurance, but without requiring actual loss or damage as a condition to settlement. Derivatives enable users not only to hedge risk, but also to benefit from advantageous price movements in the underlying assets.

Derivatives are widely used throughout the U.S. and global economies. They are used by both big and small enterprises, such as farming and ranching operations, commercial manufacturers, power utilities, retirement funds, banks and investment firms. More than 90 percent of Fortune 500 companies use derivatives to control costs and other risks in their worldwide business operations.[10]

A. Exchange-Traded and Over-the-Counter Derivatives

Derivatives generally fall into two broad categories: exchange-traded and OTC. Exchange-traded derivatives, such as futures, are relatively fungible products with standardized terms and conditions, such as delivery locations and expiration dates, and uniform trading and credit procedures. Exchange-traded markets are generally domestic or national markets. In the U.S., futures exchanges called designated contract markets (DCMs)[11] facilitate the execution of futures products mostly through anonymous central limit order books (*i.e.*, CLOBs or trading facilities).[12] Exchange-traded futures must be cleared through a CCP, which in the U.S. regulatory framework is generally

---

[9] Robert J. Shiller, Finance and the Good Society 76 (Princeton University Press 2012) (Shiller). Shiller cites Aristotle's *Politics* description of the successful use of options on olive pressing by the Greek philosopher Thales in the mid-620s to mid-540s BCE.
[10] Anatoli Kuprianov, *2009 ISDA Derivatives Usage Survey*, International Swaps and Derivatives Association (ISDA) Research Notes, No. 2, at 1-5 (Spring 2009), *available at* http://www.isda.org/researchnotes/pdf/ISDA-Research-Notes2.pdf.
[11] 17 C.F.R. 1.3(a) and (h).
[12] CEA section 1a(51); 7 U.S.C. 1a(51).

contractually tied to the DCM that lists the product, and also integrates data reporting, trade confirmation and settlement in its range of services.

In contrast to exchange-traded futures, OTC derivatives, such as swaps,[13] are far less fungible. Swaps range from highly customized structures with long maturities to somewhat more liquid and standardized instruments with shorter maturities. OTC derivatives come in a broad array of unique instruments that are almost infinitely variable in their terms. In its 2014 annual survey,[14] *Risk Magazine* identified over seventy OTC derivative categories in a range of asset classes.[15] Swaps trading is a global activity that takes place in numerous cross-jurisdiction liquidity pools through competing execution and clearing venues in global trading centers, such as New York, London, Singapore and Hong Kong. An increasing number of OTC swaps are cleared through a CCP. However, many swaps are bilateral, privately negotiated agreements.

A comparison of the respective notional amounts outstanding in the OTC and exchange-traded derivatives markets highlights the importance of OTC products. As of June 2014, the notional outstanding amount of exchange-traded derivatives was $29 trillion, whereas the notional outstanding amount of OTC derivatives was 24 times that size at $691 trillion.[16] Exchange-traded derivatives thus accounted for less than 5 percent of the total outstanding global derivatives transactions, with the remainder being OTC derivatives.[17]

Futures and swaps are complementary product sets that work symbiotically to provide accurate and effective risk hedging and mitigation. They are often used

---

[13] A swap is an agreement between two parties to exchange cash flows or other assets or liabilities at specified payment dates during the agreed-upon life of the contract.

[14] Tom Osborn, *Bank Rankings 2014: a question of scale*, Risk.net (Sep. 2, 2014), available at *http://www.risk.net/risk-magazine/research/2362542/bank-rankings-2014-a-question-of-scale*.

[15] The survey covered 73 derivatives categories, including (a) interest rate swaps (IRS) in major currencies, such as U.S. Dollar, Euro and Japanese Yen, (b) credit swaps, such as credit index default swaps (CDS) and (c) foreign exchange (FX) swaps in the major currency pairs. Swaps are also widely used for a broad range of commodities, such as oil, coal, electric power, natural gas, industrial and precious metals and other commodities, and for the transportation and storage thereof.

[16] *International Banking and Financial Market Developments*, Bank for International Settlements (BIS) Quarterly Review, Statistical Annex, Table 23A (Dec. 2014), *available at* https://www.bis.org/publ/qtrpdf/r_qa1412.pdf.

[17] *Id.* at Table 19.

together. As noted, futures have standardized terms and durations that make them well-suited to hedge generalized risks. However, futures products alone cannot address the risk-hedging needs of commercial enterprises in a highly sophisticated global economy.[18] To more effectively hedge less standardized risks over longer durations and larger exposures, swaps are used alone or in conjunction with standardized futures products. Without the customized hedging that swaps afford, commercial entities would have no choice but to accept basis risk.[19] Properly using futures and swaps effectively limits commercial basis risk, thus controlling costs and freeing up capital to invest in new enterprises or additional employment, among other initiatives, promoting economic growth.

B. Different Liquidity and Trading Characteristics

Any assessment of the effectiveness of swaps trading regulations must begin with an appreciation of the unique nature of swaps trading liquidity because liquidity determines most other aspects of the global swaps market structure, including the roles of trading participants, support infrastructure, methods of execution and clearing and product development.

In essence, liquidity is the degree to which a financial instrument may be easily bought or sold with minimal price disturbance. The liquidity of a market for a particular financial instrument depends on several factors, including product demand and scarcity, the number of market participants and facilitators of liquidity, the number of bids and offers, the size of bid-offer spreads and the volume of trading activity. These factors derive from the particular characteristics of a financial instrument, including product

---

[18] Using a simple analogy, the marketplace for hedging the complex commercial needs of the $17 trillion U.S. economy may be seen as a balloon. One end of the balloon consists of the large OTC swaps market, and the other end consists of the smaller exchange-traded futures market. Together, the balloon is in balance. Regulatory efforts to squeeze the large swaps end of the balloon may succeed in pushing some trading into the smaller futures end. Squeezing a little may be okay. Squeezing too much will strain the futures end of the balloon. Squeezing too much will burst it.

[19] Basis risk is defined as "the risk that the value of a hedge will not move exactly inversely to the value of the asset or liability being hedged," a risk which "arises from the imperfect match between the characteristics of the hedge vehicle and the item being hedged." Edward D. Kleinbard, *Competitive Convergence in the Financial Services Markets*, 81 Taxes: The Tax Magazine, at 225, 258 n.166 (Mar. 2003).

parameters such as tenor and duration and the degree of standardization of an instrument's terms.

Liquidity in the swaps market is fundamentally different than liquidity in the futures and equities markets. Generally, liquidity in the swaps market is episodic in nature as compared with liquidity in the futures and equities markets, which is continuous in nature.[20] In 2011, the Federal Reserve Bank of New York (New York Fed) published an analysis of CDS transactions over a three-month period in 2010.[21] The New York Fed's analysis demonstrated that the vast majority of single-name CDS contracts traded less than *once* per day and index CDS contracts traded less than ten times per day, but in very large sizes.[22] In a similar analysis of IRS transactions, the New York Fed estimated that the vast majority of IRS contracts traded only once during the three-month period studied.[23] Such episodic liquidity can often be volatile, with liquidity peaks and troughs that are seasonal (*e.g.,* certain energy products in extremely cold winter weather) or tied to external market and economic conditions (*e.g.,* interest rate products in response to central bank tightening or loosening of interest rates).

The episodic nature of swaps liquidity results is characteristic of markets that feature a limited number of counterparties, almost all of which are relatively large

---

[20] The distinct nature of swaps liquidity has been the subject of several well-researched studies and comment letters presented to the CFTC and the Securities and Exchange Commission (SEC). *See, e.g., Block Trade Reporting for Over-the-Counter Derivatives Markets,* ISDA and Securities Industry and Financial Markets Association (SIFMA) (Jan. 18, 2011) (ISDA/SIFMA Block Trade Study), *available at* http://www.isda.org/speeches/pdf/Block-Trade-Reporting.pdf; J.P. Morgan Comment Letter to Real-Time Public Reporting of Swap Transaction Data Proposed Rule (Jan. 12, 2011), *available at* http://comments.cftc.gov/PublicComments/ViewComment.aspx?id=27106&SearchText=j.p.%20morgan.

[21] Kathryn Chen et al., *An Analysis of CDS Transactions: Implications for Public Reporting,* Federal Reserve Bank of New York, Staff Report no. 517 (Sep. 2011), *available at* http://www.newyorkfed.org/research/staff_reports/sr517.pdf.

[22] *Id.* at 12-14. The New York Fed's analysis also revealed that the most active single-name CDS contracts only traded a little over twenty times per day, and the most active index CDS contracts only traded over 100 times per day. *Id.* at 12.

[23] Michael Fleming et al., *An Analysis of OTC Interest Rate Derivatives Transactions: Implications for Public Reporting,* Federal Reserve Bank of New York, Staff Report No. 557, at 14 (Mar. 2012 rev. Oct. 2012), *available at* http://www.newyorkfed.org/research/staff_reports/sr557.pdf (discussing episodic liquidity in the IRS market) ("Even the most commonly traded instruments in our data set were not traded with a high degree of frequency. In fact, no single instrument in the IRS data set traded more than 150 times per day, on average, and the most frequently traded instruments in OIS and FRA only traded an average of 25 and four times per day, respectively."). *Id.* at 3. *See also* ISDA/SIFMA Block Trade Study at 13-21.

institutions. The swaps market is generally closed to retail investors and under U.S. law is only open to eligible contract participants.[24] On any given day in these markets, large institutional counterparties conduct only a few thousand transactions in very large notional amounts for a broad array of unique instruments that are almost infinitely variable in their terms.

In contrast, many exchange-traded markets, such as certain equities and futures, have relatively continuous liquidity. In these markets, buyers and sellers actively submit orders leading to high transaction flow. As a result, tens of thousands of trades take place each day in many exchange-traded instruments. For example, certain Eurodollar futures contracts trade on the Chicago Mercantile Exchange (CME) over 375,000 times per day.[25] Exchange-traded markets, however, offer no guarantee of trading liquidity, as evidenced by the high percentage of new exchange-listed products that regularly fail to enjoy active trading.

The relatively continuous liquidity results from markets that feature a broad range of customers, including retail customers, who trade generally small-sized orders for a more limited range of highly fungible instruments based on standard characteristics and a few key measures or parameters (e.g., price and size). Exchange-traded markets feature substantial price competition, tighter bid-offer spreads and high trading volume that further fuel their liquidity.

The following chart provides a generalized comparison of the liquidity and trading characteristics of the swaps and futures markets:

---

[24] CEA section 1a(18); 7 U.S.C. 1a(18). The Commodity Exchange Act (CEA) limits "eligible contract participants" to institutional investors, such as investment firms, insurers, commodity pools and large employee-benefit plans. *Id.*

[25] *E.g.,* CME Eurodollar futures contract December 2015 expiration, average daily volume, week ending Jan. 9, 2015, *available at* http://www.cmegroup.com/trading/interest-rates/stir/eurodollar_quotes_volume_voi.html?optid=1#tradeDate=20150109 (last accessed Jan. 12, 2015).

Generalized Comparison of OTC Swaps Market to Exchange-Traded Futures Market[26]		
Characteristic	**Listed Futures**	**OTC Swaps**
Trade Size	Small	Very, very large
Tradable Products	1,000s	100,000s[27]
Daily Trading Volume	100,000s	100s
Trading Counterparties	100,000s (including retail)	Dozens (no retail)

The difference between swaps and futures markets has been likened to two pyramids – one upside down and one right-side up.[28] In each case, the base of the pyramid is the number of participants in a market and the ceiling is the average trade size and number of instruments traded.[29] The swaps market pyramid has a narrow base, but a very broad point, while the futures market pyramid has a broad base and a narrow point.[30]

C. Different Market Structures

It is because of the episodic liquidity in many of the swaps markets that they have generally evolved over the past several decades into two-tiered marketplaces for institutional market participants, that is, "dealer-to-customer" (D2C) marketplaces and "dealer-to-dealer" (D2D) marketplaces.

---

[26] *See* ISDA/SIFMA Block Trade Study at 13-15.
[27] Inclusive of all tenors, strikes and duration.
[28] Joe Rennison, *Interdealer Broker Rankings 2014: Sef Questions Piling Up*, Risk.net, Sep. 2, 2014, *available at* http://www.risk.net/risk-magazine/research/2362397/interdealer-broker-rankings-2014-sef-questions-piling-up (quoting Chris Ferreri of ICAP PLC) (Rennison).
[29] *Id.*
[30] *Id.*

In D2C marketplaces, corporate end-users of swaps and other buy-side traders recognize the risk that, at any given time, a particular swaps market will not have sufficient liquidity to satisfy their need to acquire or dispose of swaps positions. As a result, these liquidity "taking" counterparties turn to sell-side dealers and other market makers (*i.e.,* liquidity makers) with large balance sheets that are willing to take on the liquidity risk for a fee. These buy-side-to-sell-side transactions are known in the swaps industry as dealer-to-customer or D2C transactions.

From a market structure standpoint, liquidity takers benefit from D2C liquidity makers acting in a competitive environment. The liquidity makers compete with each other, often deriving small profits per trade from a large volume of transactions. By relying on their ability to deploy capital to make markets and using their distribution and professional knowledge to offer competitive prices to their customer base, sell-side dealers and other market makers provide essential liquidity to these customers for hedging and other risk-management strategies.

In D2D marketplaces, sell-side dealers have access to marketplaces operated by wholesale and interdealer brokers for the secondary trading of their swaps exposure. These wholesale marketplaces allow dealers to almost instantly hedge the market risk of their large swaps inventory by trading with other primary dealers and sophisticated market-making participants. In this way, these wholesale markets are similar to upstairs block markets in stocks or off-exchange block trading in futures for large-sized trades. These transactions are known in the swaps industry as dealer-to-dealer or D2D transactions.

Dealers price their customer trades based on the cost of hedging those trades in D2D markets. Without access to D2D markets, the risk inherent in holding swaps inventory arguably would require dealers to charge their buy-side customers much higher prices for taking on their liquidity risk, assuming they remained willing to do so.

In contrast, in futures markets, continuous liquidity and broad market participation mean participants generally face much lower liquidity risk. As a result, buy-side customers and market makers generally operate in the same market, leading to an all-to-all market structure, with some exceptions where there are price and liquidity risk concerns, such as for large-size block trades.[31]

Further, as mentioned above, in exchange-traded futures markets the exchange generally integrates data reporting, trade confirmation and settlement in its range of services. Swaps markets, on the other hand, are served by a range of often independent, third-party commercial service providers for trade data reporting, affirmation and confirmation. This design is a function of the fact that swaps products are not the exclusive intellectual property of any particular execution venue, as explained in Section I.E. below. Therefore, execution platforms do not know or have access to all of a product's terms and are not designed to handle these post-trade processing functions. Third-party service providers have stepped in to fulfill these essential functions.

Similarly, swaps markets support third-party vendors that provide compression, risk reduction, risk recycling, dynamic hedging and other services that seek to reduce counterparties' outstanding trade count, outstanding notional value or risk exposures.[32] These services provide innovative solutions for participants to help them achieve operational efficiencies in managing their swaps portfolios and to reduce systemic risk. These services exist in the swaps market given the non-standardized terms and conditions of swaps products, such as unique termination dates, coupon rates and notional amounts that make it operationally challenging to offset risk. This situation exists to a far lesser extent in the futures market given futures products' standardized terms and conditions.

---

[31] In such cases, third-party introducing brokers may arrange block trades off the centralized market and then enter the trades into the exchange on a delayed basis for settlement and clearing purposes. This is analogous to the swaps market, where there are non-CLOB execution methods given the liquidity risk concerns and large-size transactions.

[32] See Core Principles and Other Requirements for Swap Execution Facilities, 78 FR 33,476, 33,480-483 (Jun. 4, 2013) (SEF Rule) (discussing portfolio compression and risk mitigation services).

D. Different Methods of Trade Execution

The episodic liquidity of the swaps market has given rise to a broad and diverse range of competing venues with multiple methods of trade execution.

In D2C markets, dealers and other market makers traditionally interact directly with their institutional investor and end-user clients through telephone, email or text message communications. Increasingly, participants conduct transactions through multi-dealer-to-institutional-investor electronic trading platforms. These platforms contain request for quote (RFQ) protocols, where a buy-side liquidity taker may request and act upon live price quotes for the purchase or sale of specified swap products in specified quantities from multiple sell-side dealers and other liquidity makers. Such RFQ platforms may be one-to-one or one-to-multiple trade execution facilities.

In D2D markets, intermediaries known as interdealer brokers arrange trades between dealer participants. They gain access (almost on a consignment-like basis) to sell-side dealers' inventory of swaps products and solicit interest and negotiate transactions in such inventory with other dealers. In such markets, execution methods and techniques vary widely according to product trading characteristics along the continuum of swaps market liquidity from low-to-high. In almost all cases, interdealer broker platforms may be characterized as multiple-to-multiple trade execution facilities.

For less standardized swaps markets, where liquidity is not continuous and negotiation is common, wholesale trading platforms often feature voice execution that is similar to traditional "open-outcry" trading pits. On these platforms, professional brokerage personnel communicate bids and offers to counterparties in real time through a combination of electronic display screens and hundreds of always-open phone lines, as well as email and text messages.

In other slightly more standardized swaps markets, venues provide, for example, (a) hybrid modes of broker "work-up," where brokers broadcast completed trades to the market in order to attract other participants to "join the trade" to increase trading volume[33] and (b) time-limited, batch auction-based methods or Dutch Auction methods, such as fixing and matching sessions, where multiple participants place bids or offers on a specific product in an abbreviated timeframe in order to determine a market price or quantity.[34]

Finally, in a few, more continuously liquid swaps markets, wholesale swaps trading venues operate electronic order book platforms. In every case, a trading platform's technology and execution methodology calibrate to the particular liquidity characteristics of the instruments traded and disseminate customer bids and offers to the widest extent possible to foster the greatest degree of trading liquidity.

The distinct trade execution methods used in D2C markets and D2D markets are not unprecedented in the world of finance. They have corollaries in the long-established U.S. government-bond and corporate fixed-income markets, both of which serve U.S. and global capital markets. In these markets, approximately 50 percent of government bonds and 80 percent of credit markets and corporate bonds are negotiated and traded telephonically.[35] This method of execution differs markedly from the generally all-to-all market structure of the U.S. futures markets, where the telephone is increasingly rare.

Returning to the analogy of the two pyramids, futures markets in the form of a right-side up pyramid, with many participants trading a small set of standardized instruments, more readily support electronic CLOB trading. On the other hand, swaps markets, represented by the inverted pyramid, with a relatively small number of participants trading a wide variety of non-standardized products, tend to support one-to-

---

[33] *See, e.g.,* Wholesale Markets Brokers' Association Americas (WMBAA) Comment Letter to SEF Rule (Aug. 1, 2012), *available at* http://comments.cftc.gov/PublicComments/ViewComment.aspx?id=58343&SearchText=. During a broker "work-up," for a period of time after an order is executed, the price of the transaction is reported to the market and any market participant may engage in transactions in that asset at a price matching that of the original order so long as parties interested in counter-trading remain available. *See id.*
[34] *See, e.g.,* WMBAA Comment Letter to SEF Rule, at 3 (Jul. 18, 2011), *available at* http://comments.cftc.gov/PublicComments/ViewComment.aspx?id=47865&SearchText=wholesale.
[35] Hirander Misra, *Fixed Income Robot Wars & the Rise of the Machines,* TABB FORUM, Nov. 18, 2014, *available at* http://tabbforum.com/opinions/fixed-income-robot-wars-and-the-rise-of-the-machines.

multiple voice and electronic RFQ protocols in D2C markets and multiple-to-multiple voice- and auction-based protocols in D2D markets.[36]

It is noteworthy that while algorithmic trading and high-frequency trading (HFT) are an increasing presence in U.S. futures markets, they are generally absent from global swaps markets. This distinction proceeds from the different methods of execution prevalent in the two markets. The mandatory continuous CLOB model in U.S. futures markets and U.S. equity markets accommodates and, arguably,[37] rewards algorithmic trading and HFT strategies and methodologies. On the other hand, traditional swaps execution methods, such as electronic RFQ, voice execution and time-limited, batch auctions do not readily accommodate algorithmic trading or HFT.

E. **Different Process of Product Development**

Swaps products generally develop in a different manner than do futures products. Sell-side dealers generally create new and novel swaps products as OTC bilateral contracts with their buy-side customers. Such new derivative instruments often have distinctive terms and little or no trading history with which to estimate price. They generally begin to trade on platforms only after they have gained sufficient trading liquidity so that dealer firms need to access a secondary market to offset their primary market exposure to the product.

The structure and terms of most swaps products may be likened to an "open-source" design permitting their broad usage in global markets. Because swaps products are not the exclusive intellectual property of any particular execution venue, they may and often do transact on numerous platforms. Since no one platform owns a swap product or asserts exclusive right to execute it, trading platforms do not know or have access to all of the terms and corresponding documentation that the buy-side customers and sell-side dealers created. In short, swaps products move to platforms

---

[36] Rennison.

[37] Eric Budish et al., *The High-Frequency Trading Arms Race: Frequent Batch Auctions as a Market Design Response*, (Dec. 23, 2013), *available at* http://faculty.chicagobooth.edu/eric.budish/research/HFT-FrequentBatchAuctions.pdf; Eric Budish et al., *Presentation to the CFTC's Technology Advisory Committee*, (Feb. 10, 2014), *available at* http://www.cftc.gov/ucm/groups/public/@newsroom/documents/file/tac021014_budish.pdf.

generally after they are successful, not before. They never become the exclusive intellectual property of any trading venue.[38]

Futures products, in contrast, begin and end life directly on the exchange. The product is the proprietary intellectual property of the exchange that spent time and resources to develop it. It is, in other words, "closed-source." Many new futures products never attract liquidity. Those that do may only trade on the exchange that owns the product and controls the product's terms and conditions. Futures products are generally launched on the exchange before their success is assured and before they have attracted any trading liquidity.

---

[38] A hypothetical example will help to illustrate this point. A buy-side client who operates a wind farm approaches a dealer to create a swap to hedge its wind exposure. The sell-side dealer creates and executes a customized wind swap with its buy-side client. As time progresses, additional buy-side clients with wind exposure approach their dealers to create similar swaps. Once a critical mass of dealers are serving customers seeking such wind swaps, the dealers need a secondary market to trade in and out of this exposure. At this point, a platform or interdealer broker comes along to provide this secondary market for wind swaps. The swap product will generally trade on several wholesale platforms and, in time, may be featured on one or more dealers' direct D2C platforms.

II.   THE DODD-FRANK SWAPS TRADING REGULATORY FRAMEWORK

If firms and individuals cannot insure themselves against bad outcomes, they will be necessarily cautious; the economy will grow more slowly than it should. A company will not invest in a new factory, if it cannot hedge against swings in exchange rates that might render its investment unprofitable. An individual will not consume to the full extent of his capacity if he cannot insure his house or health. By connecting the ranks of insurance seekers with specialists who pool risk and so reduce it, finance liberates animal spirits and boosts prosperity.[39]

While a full assessment of the social utility of swaps, futures and other derivatives products is beyond the scope of this White Paper, it is generally well accepted that derivatives serve the needs of society to control commercial and other risk.[40] They are essential to U.S. economic growth and job creation.[41] American Nobel Laureate and economist Robert J. Shiller explains that in free market economic systems, complex markets have evolved, such as those for equities, bonds, futures, swaps and insurance that allow business owners to shift a portion of the risk of uncertainty.[42] The benefit of risk-shifting is that risks are transferred to the party best able to bear them through its wealth and ability to pool risks.[43] Markets for risk-shifting enable productive but higher-risk activities that investors would not otherwise undertake.[44]

Whether one accepts or rejects such arguments for the social utility of derivatives, two things are incontrovertible. The first is that faced with the opportunity to

---

[39] Sebastian Mallaby, *Sunday Book Review: Finance and the Good Society, by Robert J Shiller*, The New York Times, Jun. 22, 2012, *available at* http://www.nytimes.com/2012/06/24/books/review/finance-and-the-good-society-by-robert-j-shiller.html?pagewanted=all&_r=0.

[40] Shiller at 75-80.

[41] The Milken Institute found the following economic benefits to the U.S. economy from derivatives: "Banks' use of derivatives, by permitting greater extension of credit to the private sector, increased U.S. quarterly real GDP by about $2.7 billion each quarter from Q1 2003 to Q3 2012; derivatives use by non-financial firms increased U.S. quarterly real GDP by about $1 billion during the same period by improving the firms' ability to undertake capital investments; combined, derivatives expanded U.S. real GDP by about $3.7 billion each quarter; the total increase in U.S. economic activity was 1.1 percent ($149.5 billion) between 2003 and 2012; by the end of 2012, use of derivatives boosted U.S. employment by 530,400 (0.6 percent) and industrial production 2.1 percent." Apanard Prabha et al., *Deriving the Economic Impact of Derivatives*, Milken Institute, at 1 (Mar. 2014), *available at* http://assets1b.milkeninstitute.org/assets/Publication/ResearchReport/PDF/Derivatives-Report.pdf.

[42] Shiller at 75-80.

[43] *See generally* Kenneth J. Arrow, *Insurance, Risk and Resource Allocation* (1971) in Essays in the Theory of Risk-Bearing 134-143 (Markham Pub. Co. 1971).

[44] *Id.*

abolish or restrict the use of derivatives as a matter of U.S. law, Congress did not do so under the Dodd-Frank Act. Thus, one can assume that Congress was satisfied that an acceptable degree of social utility is inherent to derivatives. The second is that whatever social and commercial value derivatives provide, exchange-traded futures do not provide such value in materially greater measure as compared with OTC swaps. Certainly, Congress did not draw such a distinction. Congress could have restricted derivatives use to exchange-traded futures or required swaps to trade exclusively on DCMs. Congress did not take that step. Congress could also have subjected swaps to a futures-like execution model in contravention of the way swaps actually trade in global markets. Fortunately, Congress did not do that either. Instead, Congress laid out a fairly simple and flexible swaps trading framework suited to the episodic nature of swaps liquidity.

In essence, Title VII of the Dodd-Frank Act requires execution of most cleared swaps on DCMs or registered swap execution facilities (SEFs) via a straightforward trade execution requirement.[45]

Congress expressly permitted SEFs to offer various flexible execution methods for swaps transactions using "any means of interstate commerce." The law defines a SEF as a "trading system or platform in which multiple participants have the ability to execute or trade swaps by accepting bids and offers made by multiple participants in the facility or system, through any means of interstate commerce, including any trading facility, that – (A) facilitates the execution of swaps between persons; and (B) is not a designated contract market."[46]

Additionally, Congress articulated goals, not requirements, for this SEF framework in order to maintain its flexibility. Congress set two goals for SEFs in Title VII of the Dodd-Frank Act: to promote (1) the trading of swaps on SEFs and (2) pre-trade price transparency in the swaps market.[47]

---

[45] CEA section 2(h)(8); 7 U.S.C. 2(h)(8).
[46] CEA section 1a(50); 7 U.S.C. 1a(50).
[47] CEA section 5h(e); 7 U.S.C. 7b-3(e).

Congress did not prescribe that the global swaps market be carved into an isolated U.S. domestic market and then further sliced and diced into smaller and smaller domestic markets for swaps trading.[48]

Congress mandated "impartial" access to swaps markets, not "open" access. It did not require SEFs to merge D2C and D2D market segments. Indeed, in providing that a SEF must establish rules to provide market participants with impartial access to the market, the Dodd-Frank Act requires a SEF to set out any limitation on this access.[49] This requirement confirms that the Act does not demand that all market participants receive access to every market. There is no mandate or impetus for an all-to-all swaps market structure in the Dodd-Frank Act.

Congress further laid out a core principles-based framework for SEFs and provided them with reasonable discretion to comply with these principles.[50]

In crafting Title VII of the Dodd-Frank Act, Congress got much of it right.[51] Unfortunately, the CFTC's implementation of the swaps trading rules widely misses the congressional mark.

---

[48] *See* Sections III.A. and B. and IV.A. and B.
[49] CEA section 5h(f)(2); 7 U.S.C. 7b-3(f)(2).
[50] CEA section 5h(f)(1)(B); 7 U.S.C. 7b-3(f)(1)(B).
[51] The Dodd-Frank Act missed the mark with respect to the SEF core principles. Most of the SEF core principles are based on the DCM core principles. *Compare* 7 U.S.C. 7(d) (enumerating DCM core principles, including enforcement of exchange rules, restricting trading to those contracts not readily subject to manipulation, monitoring of trading, ensuring accurate recordkeeping and reporting, establishing position limits, adopting rules for emergency authority, etc.), *with id.* 7b-3(f) (setting forth extremely similar core principles applicable to SEFs). However, the futures regulatory model is inappropriate for swaps trading given the different liquidity and market structure characteristics of swaps. *See* Sections I. and III.H. for further details.

III. THE CFTC'S FLAWED SWAPS TRADING REGULATORY FRAMEWORK

Thomas Aquinas observed that the art of sailing must govern the art of shipbuilding.[52] By that, he meant that the way in which human activities are ordered and governed should be based on the ultimate good desired.[53] Hence, shipbuilding should be conducted to allow for safe and efficient navigation. Sailing should not be jeopardized by aesthetically pleasing, but unseaworthy ship designs.

So too, effective regulation should always have as its goal the betterment of the activities being regulated. Using readily available yet unsuitable frameworks in order to mollify political expectations does not produce sound regulation.

In response to political pressure to hurry the implementation of the Dodd-Frank Act and likely influenced by the naïve view that centralized order-driven markets are the best way to execute all derivatives transactions, the CFTC acted expediently and modeled its swaps trading rules on the well-known and readily available, regulatory template of the U.S. futures market. Unfortunately, that structure – though well-designed for futures – is ill-suited to global swaps trading.

The approach precluded adequate thoroughness and precision in crafting a swaps regime informed by the unique characteristics of swaps trading. As a result, the CFTC's swaps trading framework is mismatched to the natural commercial workings of the market. It is a square peg being forced into a round hole. In adopting this framework, the CFTC failed to properly respond to congressional intent and the Dodd-Frank Act's express goal of promoting swaps trading on SEFs.[54]

A. Limits on Methods of Execution

The SEF rules create two categories of swaps transactions: Required Transactions (*i.e.,* any transaction involving a swap that is subject to the trade execution

---

[52] Saint Thomas Aquinas, The Summa Contra Gentiles (The English Dominican Fathers trans., Burns Oates & Washbourne Ltd. 1924).
[53] *Id.* at Chapter I.
[54] CEA section 5h(e); 7 U.S.C. 7b-3(e).

requirement)[55] and Permitted Transactions (*i.e.,* any transaction not involving a swap that is subject to the trade execution requirement)[56] and prescribe execution methods for each category.[57] Required Transactions must be executed in an order book (Order Book)[58] or an RFQ system in which a request for a quote is sent to three participants operating in conjunction with an Order Book (RFQ System).[59] Any method of execution is allowed for Permitted Transactions,[60] but SEFs must also offer an Order Book for such transactions.[61]

There is no firm statutory support for segmenting swaps into two categories or for limiting one of those categories to two methods of execution. A footnote to the preamble of the final SEF rules justifies this segmentation by stating that Commodity Exchange Act (CEA) section 2(h)(8) "*sets out specific trading requirements* for swaps that are subject to the trade execution mandate ... [and] [t]o meet these statutory requirements, [the SEF rule] defines these swaps as Required Transactions and provides *specific methods of execution for such swaps.*"[62] The only thing that CEA section 2(h)(8) expressly requires, however, is that swaps subject to the trade execution requirement must be executed on a SEF or DCM.[63] The statute nowhere references the concept of Required Transactions with limited execution methods and Permitted Transactions via any method of execution. These artificial categories unnecessarily complicate Congress's simple and flexible swaps trading framework.

Rather, the Dodd-Frank Act's SEF definition contemplates a platform where multiple participants have the ability to execute swaps with multiple participants through any means of interstate commerce, including a trading facility.[64] Congress clearly

---

[55] 17 C.F.R. 37.9(a)(1).
[56] 17 C.F.R. 37.9(c)(1).
[57] 17 C.F.R. 37.9(a)(2) and 37.9(c)(2).
[58] 17 C.F.R. 37.3(a)(2), 37.3(a)(3), and 37.9(a)(2).
[59] 17. C.F.R. 37.9(a)(2) and 37.9(a)(3).
[60] 17 C.F.R. 37.9(c)(2).
[61] 17 C.F.R. 37.3(a)(2); SEF Rule at 33,504.
[62] SEF Rule at 33,493 n. 216 (emphasis added). The Commission further stated, to "distinguish these swaps from other swaps that are not subject to the trade execution mandate, [the SEF rule] defines such swaps ... as Permitted Transactions and allows these swaps to be voluntarily traded on a SEF by using any method of execution." *Id.*
[63] CEA section 2(h)(8); 7 U.S.C. 2(h)(8).
[64] CEA section 1a(50); 7 U.S.C. 1a(50).

drafted this broad and flexible definition to allow execution methods beyond an Order Book or RFQ System for all swaps, not just some swaps. In this regard, the CFTC Order Book obligation is not supported by the statutory text that contains a multiple-to-multiple participant trading requirement, not an all-to-all trading requirement.

Dodd-Frank also permits SEFs to offer swaps trading "through any means of interstate commerce." The SEF rules acknowledge this phrase but construe it narrowly to allow for voice and other "means" of execution or communication within the limited Order Book and RFQ System execution methods.[65] Yet, the phrase "interstate commerce" has a rich constitutional history, which U.S. federal courts have interpreted to cover almost an unlimited range of commercial and technological enterprise.[66] The CFTC rule construct is disingenuous and not supported by the plain language of the statute. Rather, it expresses a bias for two specific execution methods over all others: one drawn from the all-to-all U.S. futures markets and one that is generally one-to-many not multiple-to-multiple.

Congress could have required SEFs to offer only certain limited execution methods, but chose not to take that path. Congress was well-aware of the trading facility execution method that DCMs provide for futures contracts.[67] Additionally, Congress could have preserved references to "electronic execution" included in early drafts of the Dodd-Frank Act, but decided against that narrow approach in the final statutory text in favor of the more flexible SEF definition.[68] And, while the SEF definition includes a

---

[65] 17 C.F.R. 37.9(a)(2)(ii); SEF Rule at 33,501-502. The Commission states that "in providing either one of the execution methods for Required Transactions in § 37.9(a)(2)(i)(A) or (B) of this final rulemaking (*i.e.,* Order Book or RFQ System that operates in conjunction with an Order Book), a SEF may for purposes of execution and communication use 'any means of interstate commerce,' including, but not limited to, the mail, internet, email, and telephone, provided that the chosen execution method satisfies the requirements provided in § 37.3(a)(3) for Order Books or in § 37.9(a)(3) for Request for Quote Systems." SEF Rule at 33,501.

[66] *See, e.g.,* Gonzales v. Raich, 545 U.S. 1, 17 (2005); Katzenbach v. McClung, 379 U.S. 294, 302 (1964); Wickard v. Filburn, 317 U.S. 111, 125 (1942).

[67] CEA section 1a(51); 7 U.S.C. 1a(51).

[68] *Compare* S. 3217, 111th Cong. § 720 (as reported by S. Comm. on Banking, Housing, and Urban Affairs, Apr. 15, 2010) (defining a SEF as "an electronic trading system" and discussing electronic execution of trades), *with* 7 U.S.C. 1a(50) (defining a SEF as "a trading system or platform" without reference to electronic execution).

trading facility,[69] it does not require one, nor does it limit a SEF to an Order Book or to the Commission's peculiar RFQ System definition.

It is also important to note that while execution methods of DCMs are limited by DCM Core Principle 9, which requires a competitive, open, and efficient market and mechanism that protects the price discovery process of trading in the centralized market,[70] there is no similar core principle for SEFs. The lack of such a principle for SEFs reflects Congress's understanding that swaps naturally trade through a variety of execution methods in the global marketplace given their episodic liquidity.

The preamble to the final SEF rules concedes that the statutory definition may allow for additional execution methods beyond an Order Book and RFQ System for Required Transactions.[71] It notes that a SEF may petition the CFTC for a rulemaking to include such additional methods.[72] Despite these admissions, the SEF final rules reflect a limited execution approach.[73] The SEF rules adopted this approach despite commenters' requests to allow SEFs to offer specific, additional and permissible execution methods, such as certain auction, volume match and voice broker models.[74] The SEF rules summarily reject or fail to discuss these additional execution methods.[75] There is no clear statutory justification for the conclusion that the SEF definition only allows an Order Book and RFQ System and no other execution method.[76]

---

[69] CEA section 1a(51); 7 U.S.C. 1a(51).
[70] 17 C.F.R. 38.500.
[71] SEF Rule at 33,484, 33,501.
[72] *Id.*
[73] *Id.*
[74] *See, e.g.,* WMBAA Comment Letter to SEF Rule, at 5-6 (Mar. 8, 2011), *available at* http://comments.cftc.gov/PublicComments/ViewComment.aspx?id=31296&SearchText=Wholesale; J.P. Morgan Comment Letter to SEF Rule, at 6 (Mar. 8, 2011), *available at* http://comments.cftc.gov/PublicComments/ViewComment.aspx?id=31198&SearchText=morgan; Nodal Exchange Comment Letter to SEF Rule, at 1-3 (Mar. 8, 2011), *available at* http://comments.cftc.gov/PublicComments/ViewComment.aspx?id=31234&SearchText=nodal; WMBAA Comment Letter to SEF Rule, at 2-3 (Jul. 18, 2011), *available at* http://comments.cftc.gov/PublicComments/ViewComment.aspx?id=47865&SearchText=wholesale.
[75] *See, e.g.,* WMBAA Comment Letter to SEF Rule, at 3 (Jul. 18, 2011) (The Commission failed to discuss BGC's Volume Match execution method cited in this comment letter); SEF Rule at 33,501 (rejecting blind auctions as an acceptable method of execution and rejecting all methods of execution that failed to meet the Order Book or RFQ System definitions despite the "any means of interstate commerce" language).
[76] *See, e.g.,* SEF Rule at 33,484, 33,501-502.

The preamble to the final SEF rules again and again relies on general references to the SEF definition and SEF goals to support its positions.[77] However, the general reliance on the goals of promoting pre-trade price transparency and the trading of swaps on SEFs does not justify the limited execution methods for Required Transactions.[78] Tellingly, Congress defined these as "goals," not requirements, to provide additional flexibility to the SEF framework. Assuming, for the sake of argument, that both SEF goals must be met for each SEF execution method, there are certainly other swap execution methods that would meet the SEF definition and these goals. It is hard to accept, for example, that only an RFQ system that operates in conjunction with an Order Book, where a market participant must obtain quotes from three participants who are not affiliates of each other, among other peculiar requirements, is the only RFQ system that satisfies Congress's flexible SEF definition and SEF goals.[79] A narrow interpretation of SEF execution does not comport with the broad statutory SEF definition.[80] By restricting market participants to two limited trading options, it discourages rather than promotes trading on SEFs in contravention of the express goal of the Dodd-Frank Act.[81]

The SEF rules also contain a fifteen-second time delay requirement for cross-trades through the Order Book.[82] They reference the goal of pre-trade price transparency as justification.[83] This rule provides an exception to pre-arranged trading or pre-execution communications, as long as a participant exposes the order to the market for a minimum period of time (*e.g.,* fifteen seconds).[84] The Dodd-Frank Act does not mandate such a prescriptive rule. Given the flexible SEF definition, the rules should have provided SEFs with discretion in implementing exceptions to pre-arranged trading or pre-execution communications consistent with the SEF core principles. Such a flexible approach would be consistent with congressional intent.

---

[77] *See, e.g.,* SEF Rule at 33,484, 33,496-499 and 33,501.
[78] CEA section 5h(e); 7 U.S.C. 7b-3(e).
[79] 17 C.F.R. 37.9(a)(3).
[80] CEA section 1a(50); 7 U.S.C. 1a(50).
[81] CEA section 5h(e); 7 U.S.C. 7b-3(e).
[82] 17 C.F.R. 37.9(b).
[83] SEF Rule at 33,503.
[84] 17 C.F.R. 37.9(b).

The CFTC's limited execution method approach also does not comport with the way swaps actually trade in global markets. As noted in Section I., trillions of dollars of swaps trade globally each day through a variety of execution methods designed to better account for their episodic liquidity. As such, in many cases, interdealer brokers exercise discretion in executing counterparty trades. A swap product's particular liquidity characteristics determine the execution technology and methodology, which can change over time. This liquidity continuum necessitates flexible execution methods as authorized by the Dodd-Frank Act.

CFTC swaps trading rules, however, thwart trade execution flexibility and limit needed human discretion.[85] By requiring SEFs to offer Order Books for all swaps, even very illiquid or bespoke swaps,[86] the rules embody the unsophisticated and parochial view that centralized order-driven markets, like those in the U.S. futures markets, are the best way to execute swaps transactions. That flawed view is not reflective of global swaps market reality. The unique nature of swaps trading liquidity should drive execution methods as Aquinas would have it, not the other way around. Attempts to force episodically liquid trading into centralized order-driven markets will only drive trading away. Certainly, the Dodd-Frank Act did not authorize such attempts.

The rules' misguided approach to SEF execution is showing its shortcomings. Package transactions are one example. Swaps market participants are now required to execute certain package transactions through the SEF's limited execution methods for Required Transactions.[87] Yet, many of these package transactions are ill-suited to Order Book or RFQ System execution given their limited liquidity and complex characteristics. To avoid harming swaps package trading, CFTC staff has engaged in a detailed no-action relief process for different categories of package transactions, gradually arriving upon a new "Permitted-Lite" set of execution methods in addition to

---

[85] 17 C.F.R. 37.9(a)(2).
[86] *See* SEF Rule at 33,504 (clarifying that a SEF must offer an Order Book for Permitted Transactions).
[87] Given the CFTC's definition of Required Transaction in 37.9(a)(1), a participant must execute a package transaction where one leg of the transaction is subject to the trade execution requirement through a SEF's limited execution methods in 37.9(a)(2) or break-up the package transaction and execute each leg separately. Breaking-up package transactions defeats the purpose of creating these strategies as it will increase costs and risks for participants.

the Required and Permitted methods.[88] This added complexity could have been avoided and countless hours of Commission resources could have been saved, if congressional direction that allows SEFs the flexibility to follow existing market practice and use methods of execution best matched to the existing way in which package transactions currently trade in global markets had been heeded.[89]

B. <u>Block Transactions: "Occurs Away" from SEF</u>

The CFTC block trade definition, specifically, the "occurs away" requirement, is another example of artificial segmentation like the contrived distinction between Required Transactions and Permitted Transactions. A block trade is defined as "a publicly reportable swap transaction that: (1) Involves a swap that is listed on a registered [SEF] or [DCM]; (2) 'Occurs away' from the registered [SEF's] or [DCM's] trading system or platform and is executed pursuant to the registered [SEF's] or [DCM's] rules and procedures; (3) Has a notional or principal amount at or above the appropriate minimum block size applicable to such swap; and (4) Is reported subject to the rules...."[90]

It is unclear what is being achieved by requiring block trades to be executed away from the SEF's trading platform. The "occurs away" requirement creates an arbitrary and confusing segmentation between non-block trades "on-SEF" and block

---

[88] CFTC Letter No. 14-12, *No-Action Relief from the Commodity Exchange Act Sections 2(h)(8) and 5(d)(9) and from Commission Regulation § 37.9 for Swaps Executed as Part of a Package Transaction* (Feb. 10, 2014), *available at* http://www.cftc.gov/ucm/groups/public/@newsroom/documents/letter/14-12.pdf; CFTC Letter No. 14-62, *No-Action Relief from the Commodity Exchange Act Sections 2(h)(8) and 5(d)(9) and from Commission Regulation § 37.9 for Swaps Executed as Part of Certain Package Transactions and No-Action Relief for Swap Execution Facilities from Compliance with Certain Requirements of Commission Regulations § 37.9(a)(2), § 37.203(a) and § 38.152 for Package Transactions* (May 1, 2014), *available at* http://www.cftc.gov/ucm/groups/public/@lrlettergeneral/documents/letter/14-62.pdf; and CFTC Letter No. 14-137, *Extension of No-Action Relief from the Commodity Exchange Act Sections 2(h)(8) and 5(d)(9) and from Commission Regulation § 37.9 and Additional No-Action Relief for Swap Execution Facilities from Commission Regulation § 37.3(a)(2) for Swaps Executed as Part of Certain Package Transactions* (Nov. 10, 2014), *available at* http://www.cftc.gov/ucm/groups/public/@lrlettergeneral/documents/letter/14-137.pdf.
[89] Further complicating matters, market participants have also asked questions regarding package transactions and block sizes. For example, does a package transaction qualify for block treatment if the leg of the package transaction subject to the trade execution requirement is above the block size, but the leg of the package transaction not subject to the trade execution requirement is below the block size? To date, neither the Commission nor the CFTC staff has clarified this issue in writing.
[90] 17 C.F.R. 43.2.

trades "off-SEF," especially given that a SEF may offer any method of execution for Permitted Transactions.[91] The "off-SEF" requirement also undermines the legislative goal of encouraging swaps trading on SEFs.

The block trade definition is a holdover from the futures model.[92] In futures markets, block trades occur away from the DCM's trading facility as an exception to the centralized market requirement.[93] The Commission has previously explained the rationale for this DCM exception in terms of the price risk and liquidity risk for these large-sized block trades.[94] In other words, given the generally small trade sizes for futures contracts in the centralized market and the large sizes for block trades, a counterparty executing a block trade in the centralized market would have to pay a significant price premium from the prevailing market price to execute such a large-sized order.[95]

In today's global swaps market, however, there are no "on-platform" and "off-platform" execution distinctions for certain-sized swaps trades. As explained in Section I.B., OTC swaps generally trade in very large sizes. These swaps are not constrained to CLOBs, but trade through one of a variety of execution methods appropriate to the product's trading liquidity. Thus, the same concern about the adverse market impact of large-sized trades is generally not prevalent in the swaps market.

Congress recognized these differences by not imposing on SEFs an open and competitive centralized market requirement with corresponding exceptions for certain non-competitive trades as contained in DCM Core Principle 9.[96] Congress knew that

---

[91] The CFTC's approach is also creating technological challenges for SEFs and futures commission merchants (FCMs) in facilitating pre-execution credit checks of block trades that occur way from the SEF's platform. Currently, SEFs and FCMs are unable to implement these credit checks for block trades that occur away from the SEF's platform. *See* CFTC Letter No. 14-118, *No-Action Relief for Swap Execution Facilities from Certain 'Block Trade' Requirements in Commission Regulation 43.2* (Sep. 19, 2014), *available at* http://www.cftc.gov/ucm/groups/public/@lrlettergeneral/documents/letter/14-118.pdf.
[92] *See* Alternative Executive, or Block Trading, Procedures for the Futures Industry, 64 FR 31195 (Jun. 10, 1999); Chicago Board of Trade's Proposal To Adopt Block Trading Procedures, 65 FR 58051 (Sep. 27, 2000).
[93] 17 C.F.R. 38.500.
[94] Execution of Transactions: Regulation 1.38 and Guidance on Core Principle 9, 73 FR 54097, 54099 (proposed Sep. 18, 2008).
[95] *Id.*
[96] 17 C.F.R. 38.500.

counterparties executed swaps on flexible trading platforms in very large sizes. Rather, Congress expressly authorized delayed reporting for block transactions.[97] Congress got it right. The CFTC's swaps block trade definition is inappropriate and unwarranted.

C. Unsupported Made Available to Trade Process

As noted above, Congress included a trade execution requirement in CEA section 2(h)(8) that requires SEF[98] execution for swaps subject to the clearing mandate.[99] In a simple exception to this requirement, Congress stated that this trade execution requirement does not apply if no SEF "makes the swap available to trade."[100]

CFTC rules for the made available to trade (MAT) process have proved to be unworkable and have created an unwarranted regulatory mandate around the phrase "makes the swap available to trade."[101] Under this platform-controlled MAT process, a SEF submits a MAT determination for swaps products to the Commission pursuant to part 40 of the CFTC's regulations after considering, as appropriate, certain liquidity factors for such swaps.[102] The CFTC reviews the SEF's determination, but may only deny the submission if it is inconsistent with the CEA or CFTC regulations.[103] Once MAT, these swaps are Required Transactions and counterparties must execute them on a SEF pursuant to the limited execution methods permitted by CFTC rules.[104]

---

[97] CEA section 2(a)(13)(E); 7 U.S.C. 2(a)(13)(E). Established marketplaces worldwide have long recognized that for less liquid products where a smaller number of primary dealers and market makers cross larger size transactions, the disclosure of the intention of a major institution to buy or sell could disrupt the market and lead to poor pricing. If a provider of liquidity to the market perceives greater danger in supplying liquidity, it will step away from providing tight spreads and leave those reliant on that liquidity with poorer hedging opportunities. Hence, large size or "block" trades are generally afforded a time delay before their details are reported to the marketplace.

[98] The trade execution requirement and the Commission's made available to trade process pertain to DCMs as well. Given this paper's focus on SEFs, the references to DCMs in this section have been omitted.

[99] CEA section 2(h)(8); 7 U.S.C. 2(h)(8).

[100] Id.

[101] CEA section 2(h)(8); 7 U.S.C. 2(h)(8); 17 C.F.R. 37.10, 37.12, 38.11 and 38.12; Process for a Designated Contract Market or Swap Execution Facility To Make a Swap Available to Trade, Swap Transaction Compliance and Implementation Schedule, and Trade Execution Requirement Under the Commodity Exchange Act, 78 FR 33,606 (Jun. 4, 2013) (MAT Rule).

[102] 17 C.F.R. 37.10(a), (b), 38.12(a) and (b).

[103] MAT Rule at 33,607 and 33,610. It is doubtful that the Commission could find that a MAT submission is inconsistent with the CEA or Commission regulations because neither the CEA nor the regulations contain any objective requirements that a swap must meet for a MAT determination to be valid.

[104] 17 C.F.R. 37.9(a)(1), 37.9(a)(2), 37.10, 37.12, 38.11 and 38.12.

This MAT process in combination with the CFTC's limited execution method approach is problematic for several reasons. It forces swaps to trade through a limited number of execution methods even where a product lacks the liquidity needed to support such trading. Since the MAT process is platform-controlled, a nascent SEF attempting to gain a first-mover advantage in trading liquidity may force certain swaps to trade exclusively through the SEF's restrictive methods of execution (*i.e.*, Order Book or RFQ System) before the appropriate liquidity is available to support such trading.[105] As former CFTC Commissioner Scott O'Malia stated in his dissent to the final MAT rule, an "available-to-trade determination has a far reaching effect. It binds not only the requesting SEF ... but the entire market, thus forcing all SEFs ... [that list the particular swap] to trade [it] by using more restrictive methods of execution."[106] Consequently, in creating a regulatory mandate around nothing more than the phrase "makes the swap available to trade," the MAT rule only adds a layer of bureaucratic process that lacks statutory authorization and fails to effectively guard against inadequate trading liquidity.

The Commission's MAT process is also not legally sound. As former CFTC Commissioner Scott O'Malia noted, part 40 of the CFTC's regulations does not provide an appropriate avenue for a MAT determination.[107] The Commission's rule certification and approval process under part 40 is "intended to apply to only one particular DCM or SEF that requested such rule approval or submitted such rule certification," not the entire market.[108]

The CFTC's limited execution method approach and MAT process has created an unnecessary tension between the clearing mandate and trading requirement. The determination of whether trading liquidity in an instrument is sufficient to calculate initial and variation margin to permit central clearing is a wholly different analysis than whether trading liquidity is appropriate for mandatory trade execution through an Order Book and RFQ System execution methods.

---

[105] Richard Henderson, *Numerous SEF challenges predicted in 2014*, THE TRADE, Jan. 8, 2014, *available at* http://www.thetradenews.com/news/Asset_Classes/Derivatives/Numerous_SEF_challenges_predicted_in _2014.aspx.

[106] MAT Rule at 33,632.

[107] *Id.* at 33,631.

[108] *Id.* at 33,631-632.

The current non-deliverable forward (NDF) clearing mandate debate highlights the tension between clearing and trading and the flawed swaps trading regime. At the October 9, 2014 CFTC Global Markets Advisory Committee meeting, participants noted that once NDFs are subject to the clearing mandate, the trade execution requirement is a practical certainty due to the SEF-controlled MAT process.[109] The participants voiced their concern over an NDF clearing mandate because such NDF swaps are not ready to trade pursuant to a SEF's limited execution methods.[110] Unfortunately, the ill-conceived SEF execution and MAT regime has complicated the ability to make additional clearing mandates.

All of these problems could have been avoided if flexible execution methods were permitted for all SEF trades as is plainly called for in the statutory SEF definition and the plain language was followed in CEA section 2(h)(8). If SEFs could offer flexible execution methods, then participant resistance to clearing and trading mandates would likely be diminished. Moreover, flexible SEF execution methods would eliminate the need for the unworkable and legally unsound MAT process because execution methods could be tailored to the liquidity characteristics of all swaps products. Flexible methods of execution would allow swaps trading markets to evolve rationally and organically without the forced, unwarranted and unnecessary MAT construct.

A plain reading of the trade execution requirement demonstrates that Congress did not intend to create an entire regulatory mandate around the phrase made available to trade. Unlike the clearing mandate in CEA section 2(h)(1), Congress provided no process for determining whether swaps must be traded on-SEF in CEA section 2(h)(8).[111] Congress could have instituted a regulatory mandate for the trade execution requirement as it did for the clearing mandate, but chose not to.[112] Drafters of Title VII

---

[109] *See* webcast of the October 9, 2014 Global Markets Advisory Committee meeting, *available at* http://www.cftc.gov/PressRoom/Events/opaevent_gmac100914.

[110] *Id. See also* Memorandum from Foreign Exchange Markets Subcommittee to Global Markets Advisory Committee, CFTC, Response to request for recommendation on an FX NDF mandate, at 7-9 (Dec. 5, 2014), *available at* http://www.cftc.gov/ucm/groups/public/@aboutcftc/documents/file/gmac_fxndfmandate122214.pdf (detailing issues around mandatory NDF trading).

[111] *Compare* CEA section 2(h)(1), 2(h)(2) and 2(h)(3); 7 U.S.C. 2(h)(1), 2(h)(2) and 2(h)(3), *with* CEA section 2(h)(8); 7 U.S.C. 2(h)(8).

[112] *Id.*

were aware that, unlike futures, newly developed swaps products are initially traded bilaterally and only move to a platform once trading reaches a critical stage. The trade execution requirement expresses this logic in that a clearing-mandated swap must be executed on a SEF unless no SEF makes that swap available to trade (*i.e.,* offers the swap for trading). However, congressional intent was not followed and an entire regulatory mandate was created based on nothing more than the phrase "makes the swap available to trade" in CEA section 2(h)(8).

D. Beyond Impartial Access

Congress required SEFs to have rules to provide market participants with impartial access to the market and to establish rules regarding any limitation on access.[113] The Commission, through the preamble to the final SEF rules, and staff appear to view these provisions as requiring SEFs to serve every type of market participant in an all-to-all market structure.[114] Given the Dodd-Frank Act's reference to *limitations* on access, however, efforts to require SEFs to serve every type of market participant or operate all-to-all marketplaces are unsupported by law.

There is no mandate for an all-to-all swaps market structure in the Dodd-Frank Act. Congress knew that there were D2C and D2D swaps markets before the Dodd-Frank Act, just as there are in many other mature financial markets. This structure is driven by the unique liquidity characteristics of the underlying swaps products.[115] This dynamic has not changed post-Dodd-Frank, and the law's impartial access provisions do not require or support the alteration of the present swaps market structure.[116]

The Dodd-Frank Act does not prohibit SEFs from serving separate D2D and D2C markets. Its impartial access requirement must not be confused with open access. Impartial access, as the Commission noted in the preamble to the final SEF rules,

---

[113] CEA section 5h(f)(2); 7 U.S.C. 7b-3(f)(2).
[114] SEF Rule at 33,507-508.
[115] *See* Section I.C.
[116] In a McKinsey report, an overwhelming majority of buy-side participants interviewed acknowledged the important role that dealers play in providing liquidity and were "not interested in disintermediating dealers...." *The Brave New World of SEFs: How Broker-Dealers Can Protect Their Franchises*, McKinsey & Company, Working Papers on Corporate & Investment Banking No. 4, at 5-6 (Jun. 2014) (McKinsey Working Paper)

means "fair, unbiased, and unprejudiced" access.[117] This means that SEFs should apply this standard to their participants; it does not mean that SEFs are forced to serve every type of market participant in an all-to-all futures-style marketplace. Only Congress could have imposed this mandate; it chose not to do so. Even the CFTC acknowledged in the preamble to the final SEF rules that a SEF may operate different markets and may establish different access criteria for each of its markets.[118] This preamble language and the statutory language regarding "any limitation on access" are meaningless if CFTC staff act under the supposition that SEFs are required to serve all types of market participants.

E. Unwarranted Void *Ab Initio*

Under pressure to ban breakage agreements[119] between parties,[120] the staffs of the Division of Clearing and Risk and the Division of Market Oversight (the Divisions) issued guidance that states that "any [swap] trade that is executed on a SEF … and that is not accepted for clearing should be void *ab initio*" (*i.e.*, invalid from the beginning).[121] The guidance also states that this result is consistent with CEA section 22(a)(4)(B), which prohibits participants in a swap from voiding a trade, but does not prohibit the Commission or a SEF from declaring a trade to be void.[122]

The statute does not support the Divisions' justification for this policy. Although CEA section 22(a)(4)(B) does not prohibit the Commission or a SEF from voiding a trade, it does not require this outcome if a trade is rejected from clearing.[123] This section also does not prevent a SEF from implementing rules that allow a participant to correct

---

[117] SEF Rule at 33,508.
[118] *Id.*
[119] "A breakage agreement is any arrangement, whether contained in an agreement between the parties or the rules of a SEF or DCM, that provides for the assessment of liability or payment of damages between the parties to a trade intended for clearing in the event that the trade is rejected from clearing." CFTC Letter No. 13-66, *Time-Limited No-Action Relief for Swap Execution Facilities from Compliance with Certain Requirements of Commission Regulation 37.9(a)(2) and 37.203(a)* (Oct. 25, 2013), at 4, n.13, *available at* http://www.cftc.gov/ucm/groups/public/@lrlettergeneral/documents/letter/13-66.pdf.
[120] Prior to the issuance of this guidance, the Divisions learned that certain market participants would only trade with other participants on a SEF with whom they had executed breakage agreements. These agreements dictated terms in the event a trade was rejected from clearing.
[121] Staff Guidance on Swaps Straight-Through-Processing (Sep. 26, 2013), *available at* http://www.cftc.gov/ucm/groups/public/@newsroom/documents/file/stpguidance.pdf.
[122] *Id.*
[123] CEA section 22(a)(4)(B); 7 U.S.C. 25(a)(4)(B).

errors and resubmit a trade for clearing.[124] If the Divisions' main concern is breakage agreements, there are less onerous and more direct ways to prevent such agreements.

The CFTC staff's void *ab initio* policy creates a competitive disadvantage for the U.S. swaps market relative to the U.S. futures market. There are legitimate reasons, such as operational or clerical errors, that cause swaps trades to be rejected from clearing. Even the Divisions recognized some of these legitimate reasons in their expired no-action letter that allowed certain swaps trades to be resubmitted after being rejected from clearing.[125] In the futures market, DCMs have implemented rules to address the situation where an executed futures transaction is rejected from clearing.[126] SEFs, like DCMs, would suffer from reputational risk if too many trades were rejected from clearing and no transparent, workable resolution process existed. Thus, SEFs, like DCMs, have an incentive to get clearing right and implement clear, workable error trade policies.

Furthermore, the void *ab initio* policy introduces additional risk into the system. For example, after a participant executes a swap, the participant enters into a series of other swaps to hedge its risk. If the first swap is declared void *ab initio* and there is no opportunity to resubmit the trade, then the participant will not be correctly hedged, which creates additional market and execution risk. The higher level of risk and burden to the U.S. swaps market as compared with overseas swaps markets and the U.S. futures market should not be borne without an offsetting benefit carefully considered through public notice and comment.

F. <u>Expansive Scope for Uncleared Swaps Confirmations</u>

The CFTC's approach to SEF confirmations and related agreements for uncleared swaps has been confusing and expansive in scope.

---

[124] *Id.*

[125] CFTC Letter No. 13-66, *Time-Limited No-Action Relief for Swap Execution Facilities from Compliance with Certain Requirements of Commission Regulation 37.9(a)(2) and 37.203(a)* (Oct. 25, 2013), *available at* http://www.cftc.gov/ucm/groups/public/@lrlettergeneral/documents/letter/13-66.pdf.

[126] *See, e.g.,* CME Rule 527.C. Outtrades Resolution, *available at* http://www.cmegroup.com/rulebook/CME/I/5/5.pdf; CME Rule 809.D. Reconciliation of Outtrades, *available at* http://www.cmegroup.com/rulebook/CME/I/8/8.pdf.

Under CFTC SEF rules, a SEF is required to provide "each counterparty to a transaction ... with a written record of all of the terms of the transaction which shall legally supersede any previous agreement and serve as a confirmation of the transaction."[127] Additionally, responding to comments about a SEF's confirmation for uncleared swaps, footnote 195 to the preamble of the final SEF rules states, in part, that "[t]here is no reason why a SEF's written confirmation terms cannot incorporate by reference the privately negotiated terms of a freestanding master agreement ... provided that the master agreement is submitted to the SEF ahead of execution ...."[128]

Shortly after SEFs and market participants discovered this language buried in footnote 195, they raised concerns about SEFs receiving master and other agreements, and the scope and content of the confirmation and reporting requirements applicable to uncleared swaps transactions.[129] Agency staff provided certain relief in August 2014.[130] Yet, much of the problem remains unresolved because of, among other things, a lack of clarity over which terms from an agreement must be included in SEF confirmations and subsequently reported.[131] The CFTC policy is increasing legal uncertainty, contrary to the stated goal in the preamble to the final SEF rules.[132]

The CFTC's approach to SEF confirmations is taken from the futures model. As explained in Section I.E., DCMs own their futures contracts and control the products' standardized terms. With swaps, however, SEFs do not own the products. The products' terms are akin to an "open-source" design that sell-side dealers created with their buy-side customers. Additionally, swaps market participants have long relied on master agreements, such as the International Swaps and Derivatives Association (ISDA) Master Agreement, that govern the overall trading relationship between

---

[127] 17 C.F.R. 37.6(b).

[128] SEF Rule at 33,491 n. 195.

[129] *See Request for Relief Relating to Commission Regulation Part 37 for Foreign Exchange Asset Class*, GFMA (Oct. 28, 2013), *available at* http://www.gfma.org/correspondence/item.aspx?id=4294967295; *Request for Time-Limited No-Action Relief Relating to Confirmations for Swaps Not Required or Intended to be Cleared*, SIFMA (Mar. 10, 2014), *available at* http://www.sifma.org/comment-letters/2014/sifma-submits-comments-to-the-cftc-requesting-time-limited-no-action-relief-relating-to-sef-confirmations/.

[130] CFTC Letter No. 14-108, *Staff No-Action Position Regarding SEF Confirmations and Recordkeeping Requirements under Certain Provisions Included in Regulations 37.6(b) and 45.2* (Aug. 18, 2014), *available at* http://www.cftc.gov/ucm/groups/public/@lrlettergeneral/documents/letter/14-108.pdf.

[131] *Id.*

[132] SEF Rule at 33,491.

counterparties. These master agreements set out the non-transaction specific credit and operational terms that apply to all transactions entered into under them. As a result, SEFs do not know or have access to all of these terms and corresponding documentation. This paradigm has not changed post-Dodd-Frank for uncleared swaps transactions.

Importantly, a master agreement and a confirmation serve different purposes and should be thought of as different documents. A master agreement includes provisions regarding credit and risk mitigation between counterparties, while a confirmation includes provisions regarding the limited economic terms of a particular transaction. The CFTC swap documentation rules recognize the importance and distinct purposes of these documents.[133] The rules define a master agreement as including "all terms governing the trading relationship between the [parties]"[134] and a swap confirmation as documentation that "memorializes the agreement of the counterparties to all of the terms of the *swap transaction*."[135] In other words, confirmations and master agreements are as alike as apples and oranges.

It is time to reconsider the largely illusory benefits against the almost impossible burden of requiring a SEF to confirm and report "all of the terms" of a trading relationship to which it is not a party, especially terms from agreements that do not affect the fundamental economic terms of the transaction. Without such a rethink, the SEF confirmation requirements will continue to be an obstacle for the trading of uncleared swaps on SEFs.

G. Embargo Rule and Name Give-Up

Under the embargo rule, a SEF may not disclose swap transaction and pricing data to its market participants until it transmits such data to a swap data repository (SDR) for public dissemination.[136] To effect such SDR transmission, a SEF must first enrich and convert such transaction data as required by the SDR. Alternatively, the SEF

---

[133] *Compare* 17 C.F.R. 23.501 Swap Confirmation, *with* 17 C.F.R. 23.504 Swap Trading Relationship Documentation.
[134] 17 C.F.R. 23.504(b)(1).
[135] 17 C.F.R. 23.500(c) (emphasis added).
[136] 17 C.F.R. 43.3(b)(3).

may choose to use a third-party provider to transmit data to an SDR. Only then can the SEF disclose swap transaction data to market participants on its trading platform.

The delays in transaction and pricing data disclosure caused by the embargo rule inhibit the long-established "work-up" process, whereby counterparties buy or sell additional quantities of a swap immediately after its execution on the SEF at a price matching that of the original trade.[137] It is believed that the work-up process increases wholesale trading liquidity in certain OTC swaps by as much as 50 percent.[138] The embargo rule thwarts this liquidity generation. This rule has hindered U.S. markets from continuing a well-established and crucial global trading mechanism. The effect of the embargo rule appears to prioritize public transparency – in a market that is closed to the general public[139] – at the expense of transparency for actual participants in the marketplace. It is difficult to justify this unbalanced restraint on swaps liquidity.[140]

Similarly, name give-up is a long-standing market practice in many swaps markets. With name give-up, the identities of the counterparties are disclosed to each other after they have been anonymously matched by a platform.[141] The origins of the practice lie in wholesale markets for self-cleared swaps and other products. There, counterparties to large transactions use name give-up to confirm the creditworthiness of their counterparties.

In markets with CCP clearing of swaps, however, the rationale for name give-up is less clear cut. That is because the CCP and not the trading counterparty bears the

---

[137] *See* SEF Rule at 33,500 (explaining the work-up process).

[138] Author's professional observation based on marketplace experience.

[139] The swaps market is closed to participants that are not eligible contract participants. CEA section 1a(18); 7 U.S.C. 1a(18).

[140] The preamble to the final real-time reporting rule did not respond to a public comment about the embargo rule's impact on the work-up process. Real-Time Public Reporting of Swap Transaction Data, 77 FR 1,182, 1,200-1,202 (Jan. 9, 2012).

[141] *E.g.,* After counterparties execute a swap through an anonymous order book, the identities of the counterparties are disclosed to each other. *See* Peter Madigan, *CFTC to Test Role of Anonymity in Sef Order Book Flop*, Risk.net, Nov. 21, 2014, *available at* http://www.risk.net/risk-magazine/feature/2382497/cftc-to-test-role-of-anonymity-in-sef-order-book-flop (discussing the name give-up issue) (Madigan, Anonymity); Katy Burne, *CFTC to Look Into Disclosure of Identities of Swap Counterparties*, Wall Street Journal, Nov. 12, 2014, *available at* http://www.wsj.com/articles/cftc-to-look-into-disclosure-of-identities-of-swap-counterparties-1415834947?KEYWORDS=cftc+to+look+into+disclosure+of+identities.

credit obligations. Counterparties to CCP cleared swaps primarily need assurance of each other's relation to the CCP and not the opposing counterparty's individual credit standing.

As the swaps market increasingly becomes a cleared market, it is reasonable to ask whether name give-up continues to serve a valid purpose. There are a variety of different views on both sides of this issue depending on one's position in the market. One argument against the practice of name give-up for cleared swaps is that it serves to give superior market transparency to the most active market participants at the expense of less active market participants.[142] To some experienced market observers, name give-up has been abused by major sell-side dealers to restrict participation by non-dealers and other liquidity takers in the D2D markets.[143]

A counter-argument is that, while name give-up may be less necessary for counterparty credit confirmation for cleared swaps, it remains necessary for sell-side dealer capital allocation. In other words, as bank market-making capital becomes further constrained by regulations,[144] liquidity makers need to more precisely allocate their bank capital among their customer base in coordination with their overall bank cross-marketing strategies. Without the information provided by name give-up, liquidity makers will provide less liquidity to the market, especially in times of crisis, and charge higher prices to customers.[145] This outcome arguably would hurt all market participants. Another argument is that name give-up helps to "stop market abuses."[146] According to one observer, "a predatory customer could influence the price dealers would quote via RFQ by placing an order in the Clob. If the order book is anonymous, clients might feel

---

[142] Madigan, Anonymity.
[143] *Id.* The argument is that sell-side dealers threaten to shun platforms in the D2D market that attempt to execute trades between dealers and non-dealers.
[144] *E.g.,* Due to such post-financial crisis regulatory reforms as the Volcker Rule, Basel III Accords, capital charges and other bank capital-based restrictions. *See* Anthony J. Perrotta, Jr., *An E-Trading UST Market 'Flash Crash'? Not So Fast*, TABB Group, Nov. 24, 2014, *available at* http://tabbforum.com/opinions/an-e-trading-treasury-market-'flash-crash'-not-so-fast (discussing regulatory capital constraints and declining market liquidity) (Perrotta).
[145] *See* Madigan, Anonymity; McKinsey Working Paper at 6.
[146] *See* Madigan, Anonymity.

they could play these kinds of games with impunity, so name give-up is seen as a way to keep customers honest."[147]

Some parties have urged the CFTC to ban, flat out, the practice of name give-up. Yet, there are important policy considerations on both sides of the issue that must be carefully considered before taking any action.[148] What impact would a blanket ban have on swaps market liquidity? Would such a ban cause sell-side dealers to remove liquidity from the market or charge higher prices? Would new liquidity makers fully and consistently act in the market to make up any shortfall in liquidity? Because market liquidity is increasingly recognized as a potential systemic risk to the U.S. financial system,[149] any regulatory action to curtail the use of name give-up must be thoroughly analyzed for its impact on market liquidity and systemic risk.[150]

H. Prescriptive Rules Disguised as Core Principles

Congress provided a core-principles based framework for SEFs.[151] It based this framework on the Commission's historical principles-based regulatory regime for DCMs.[152] Unfortunately, the Dodd-Frank Act missed the mark with respect to the SEF core principles, most of which are based on the DCM core principles. The successful futures regulatory model is an inappropriate template for SEF core principles.

This problem has been magnified by unwarranted amendments to CFTC rules making SEFs self-regulatory organizations (SROs)[153] and requiring them to comply with very prescriptive rules modeled after futures exchange practices that are unsuitable for the way swaps trade. Although the SEF core principles place certain regulatory obligations on SEFs, the Dodd-Frank Act does not require the CFTC to make SEFs

---

[147] *Id.*

[148] A question remains whether the CFTC has such authority under the Dodd-Frank Act.

[149] *2014 Annual Report*, Office of Financial Research, U.S. Treasury Department, at 30-33 (Dec. 2, 2014), *available at* http://www.treasury.gov/initiatives/ofr/about/Documents/OFR_AnnualReport2014_FINAL_12-1-2014.pdf.

[150] *See* Section IV.C. (discussing market liquidity risk).

[151] CEA section 5h(f); 7 U.S.C. 7b-3(f).

[152] CEA section 5(d); 7 U.S.C. 7(d) (2009); 17 C.F.R. part 38 (2009).

[153] 17 C.F.R. 1.3(ee). Adaptation of Regulations to Incorporate Swaps, 77 FR 66,288, 66,290 (Nov. 2, 2012).

SROs.[154] Additionally, it does not instruct the Commission to take a prescriptive rules-based approach to SEFs.[155] In fact, the statute provides SEFs with reasonable discretion to comply with the core principles.[156]

This approach to SEFs departs from congressional intent and the CFTC's own principles-based regulatory history in favor of prescriptive rules. As CME explained in its comment letter to the proposed SEF rule, the Commission is choosing to:

> [E]vade the principles-based regulatory regime that Congress established for SEFs in [the Dodd-Frank Act] by enacting a litany of prescriptive rules that would dictate every detail of a SEF's day-to-day operations. Had Congress wanted the Commission to abandon principles-based regulation, it certainly would not have reinforced that regime for DCMs by adding an additional five core principles and established the regulatory framework for SEFs and [SDRs] through core principles.[157]

As CME further explained, principles-based regulation has allowed U.S. DCMs to maintain a competitive position in the global market. DCMs can keep pace with rapidly changing technology and market needs, and can operate more efficiently and economically.[158] This approach is especially important for SEFs given that swaps trading volume is relatively modest as compared with futures trading volume.[159] If SEF regulatory costs are too high, only a few SEFs will be successful, and there will be a lack of competition and innovation. As explained in the next section, there is already some evidence of these negative results.[160] Congress did not intend these results when it created competitive SEFs and set a goal to promote swaps trading on these SEFs.[161]

This section explains in greater detail some of the problematic futures-based core principles and prescriptive rules.

---

[154] *Id.*
[155] CEA section 5h(f)(1)(B); 7 U.S.C. 7b-3(f)(1)(B).
[156] *Id.*
[157] CME Comment Letter to SEF Rule, at 2 (Mar. 8, 2011), *available at* http://comments.cftc.gov/PublicComments/ViewComment.aspx?id=31276&SearchText=CME.
[158] *Id.* at 2-3.
[159] *See* Section I.B.
[160] *See* Sections IV.D and E.
[161] CEA section 5h; 7 U.S.C. 7b-3.

1. Compliance with rules

SEF Core Principle 2 requires SEFs to establish and enforce compliance with rules of the SEF.[162] This core principle is based on a similar DCM core principle.[163] The departure from principles-based regulation is readily evident by reviewing the litany of prescriptive rules promulgated under the auspices of Core Principle 2. The SEF rules pursued this approach despite numerous commenters' express concerns that a prescriptive approach would harm competition and impede growth in the swaps market.[164] A few of these prescriptive rules are discussed below.

Audit trail. SEFs, like DCMs, are required to establish audit trails, which include an electronic transaction history database and electronic analysis capability with respect to all audit trail data in the database.[165] The CFTC copied verbatim most of the SEF audit trail requirements from the DCM rules.[166] In certain areas, however, the CFTC created additional burdens for SEFs as compared with DCMs. Under a SEF's electronic transaction history database requirements, a SEF must include "all indications of interest, requests for quotes, orders, and trades...."[167] This rule does not distinguish between or make allowances for electronic and non-electronic communications and execution methods commonly used in the marketplace. Under a DCM's electronic transaction history database requirements, however, for orders, a DCM only must include "*orders entered into an electronic trading system.*"[168] In the preamble to the final DCM rules, in response to a comment, the CFTC recognized this distinction between electronic trading and open-outcry trading for a DCM's audit trail rules.[169] The rationale for such a disparity between the SEF and DCM rules is not clear as the rules lack an explanation. It is clear, however, that the SEF rules add unnecessarily burdensome and

---

[162] CEA section 5h(f)(2); 7 U.S.C. 7b-3(f)(2).

[163] CEA section 5(d)(2); 7 U.S.C. 7(d)(2).

[164] SEF Rule at 33,505.

[165] 17 C.F.R. 37.205, 38.551, 38.552 and 38.553.

[166] *Compare* 17 C.F.R. 37.205 *with* 17 C.F.R. 38.551, 38.552 and 38.553.

[167] 17 C.F.R. 37.205(b)(2). As discussed earlier, the Commission permits the use of "any means of interstate commerce" in connection with the execution of Required Transactions, but only if the method of execution satisfies the Order Book or RFQ System requirements. SEF Rule at 33,484, 33,501.

[168] 17 C.F.R. 38.552(b) (emphasis added). DCMs may provide for execution through non-electronic open-outcry trading pits. CEA section 1a(51); 7 U.S.C. 1a(51).

[169] Core Principles and Other Requirements for Designated Contract Markets, 77 FR 36,612, 36,644 (Jun. 19, 2012).

costly requirements on SEFs that go beyond practices in futures and other financial markets.

The burdensome voice order database requirement for SEFs creates additional complications for SEFs in their electronic analysis capability requirements. SEFs must have the ability to electronically analyze all indications of interest, requests for quotes and orders, including through voice execution methods.[170] The preamble to the final SEF rules acknowledges that a SEF that utilizes the telephone may comply with the electronic analysis capability for oral communications by ensuring that its digital database of recordings is capable of being searched and analyzed.[171] While the SEF rules acknowledge voice execution in its audit trail discussion, SEFs that utilize voice and electronic messaging (*e.g.*, telephone and instant messaging) for execution and communication face significant challenges in complying with the electronic analysis requirements given the emergent state of voice recognition and analysis technology.[172]

Given current challenges, it appears that CFTC staff is asking SEFs to develop a surveillance program to monitor voice and electronic messages. This one-size-fits-all approach would require a SEF to review a statistically significant sample of randomly selected voice recordings and electronic messages per market participant and per SEF execution specialist to ensure compliance with electronic analysis requirements. This manually intensive process could require a SEF to review thousands and thousands of voice messages per year. The SEF rules do not contemplate such a manually intensive process.[173] Before further steps are taken to adopt such an approach, its costs must be weighed against its actual benefits.

While compliance with audit trail requirements is important, such requirements should not discourage voice execution methods for swaps given that the Dodd-Frank Act allows execution by any means of interstate commerce. For futures, the CFTC recognized differences between electronic and non-electronic execution methods for a

---

[170] 17 C.F.R. 37.205(b)(3).
[171] SEF Rule at 33,519.
[172] The author is aware of promising technology that may ease in time the cost and technological burdens associated with the ability to electronically analyze voice recordings.
[173] The CFTC did not consider the costs and benefits of such an approach in the SEF final rules. *Id.* at 33,575-577.

DCM's audit trail requirements. The same flexibility should be afforded to SEFs. In the meantime, the Commission staff should work with the SEFs to develop a better tailored approach for electronic analysis of voice transactions. For example, a SEF could target its reviews based on potentially problematic behavior discovered by the SEF or its regulatory service provider. A SEF could also target its reviews based on a number of factors, such as a SEF's business model, product listing, type of participant or volume.

Warning letters. The CFTC's approach to warning letters is also very prescriptive. Three separate CFTC rules state that no more than one warning letter may be issued by a SEF to the same person or entity found to have committed the same rule violation within a rolling twelve month period.[174] This prescriptive approach does not allow a SEF to exercise reasonable discretion to determine the appropriate action based on the totality of the circumstances. It also takes no account of the fact that many entities have supervisory oversight over hundreds of employees. The rule makes no allowances for entities and their employees to adjust to the extraordinary amount of unprecedented regulations recently and rapidly promulgated by the CFTC. Such inflexibility is unnecessarily burdensome and heavy-handed.

Supervision of regulatory service provider. The rule requiring SEFs to supervise their regulatory service providers also takes a prescriptive approach.[175] It is not necessary for the CFTC to dictate prescriptive requirements, such as holding "regular meetings" to discuss specific enumerated topics and conducting "periodic reviews" given that a SEF is always responsible for the services provided by its regulatory services provider and for compliance with its obligations under the CEA and Commission regulations.[176] The SEF and its regulatory service provider should have the flexibility to determine how to handle supervisory arrangements.

2. Monitoring of trading and trade processing

SEF Core Principle 4 requires SEFs to monitor trading in swaps to prevent manipulation, price distortion and disruptions of the delivery or cash settlement process,

---

[174] 17 C.F.R. 37.203(f)(5), 37.205(c)(2) and 37.206(f).
[175] 17 C.F.R. 37.204(b).
[176] 17 C.F.R. 37.204(a).

among other things.[177] Certain rules promulgated under Core Principle 4 require a SEF to look beyond its own market to gain the information necessary to perform these functions. For example, CFTC Regulation 37.404(a) requires a SEF to "demonstrate that it has access to sufficient information to assess whether trading in swaps listed on its market, in the index or instrument used as a reference price, or in the underlying commodity for its listed swaps is being used to affect prices on its market."[178] In other words, a SEF that executes a credit default swap on a Ford Motor Company bond must also monitor trading in the underlying Ford Motor Company bonds to prevent manipulation, price distortion and disruption in its market. While a SEF has the ability to monitor trades it executes, asking it to monitor manipulation in another marketplace in which it may provide no execution services is an undue, unfair and unwarranted burden.

The CFTC acknowledges this challenge. Its website regarding market surveillance states that only the CFTC itself can "consolidate data from multiple exchanges and foreign regulators to create a seamless, fully-surveilled marketplace" due to its unique space in the regulatory arena.[179] The surveillance "requires access to multiple streams of proprietary information from competing exchanges, and as such, can only be performed by the Commission or other national regulators."[180] The CFTC correctly states that the surveillance "cannot be filled by foreign and domestic exchanges offering related competing products,"[181] and there is no reason to believe that a SEF is better situated. And yet, despite this broad disclaimer, each SEF that fails to fulfill this sort of surveillance function will be in violation of SEF Core Principle 4 and CFTC rules.

Congress should clarify SEF Core Principle 4 to make clear that a SEF is not required to monitor markets beyond its own.[182] The Commission should also revise its

---

[177] CEA section 5h(f)(4); 7 U.S.C. 7b-3(f)(4).

[178] 17 C.F.R. 37.404(a).

[179] CFTC Market Surveillance Program, *available at* http://www.cftc.gov/IndustryOversight/MarketSurveillance/CFTCMarketSurveillanceProgram/tradepractice surveillance.

[180] *Id.*

[181] *Id.*

[182] CEA section 5h(f)(4); 7 U.S.C. 7b-3(f)(4).

rules to this effect. As the CFTC admits on its website, only the Commission can perform cross-market surveillance.

3. Position limits

SEF Core Principle 6 places the burden for position limits and position accountability levels on SEFs that are trading facilities.[183] The Dodd-Frank Act got this core principle wrong.

The setting of position limits or position accountability levels by SEFs is very problematic. As explained in Section I.E., SEFs do not own swaps products, which trade on multiple competing SEFs and bilaterally off-SEFs. SEFs lack the knowledge of a market participant's activity on and off other venues. SEFs only have information about swaps transactions that occur on their platforms, and, thus, do not know whether a particular transaction on their platform adds to, or offsets all or part of, a participant's existing position. Therefore, SEFs are not able to calculate the total position of a market participant or monitor it against any position limit. As explained in the Core Principle 4 discussion above, only a markets regulator, such as the CFTC, that has a full picture of the market can perform cross-market monitoring and surveillance functions. Position limit monitoring and surveillance is another such area.

Congress should revise Core Principle 6 to reflect that the CFTC, or possibly a designee, should set and monitor swaps position limits or accountability levels. Until Congress revises this futures-based core principle, the Commission staff should continue to work with SEFs to derive a solution that ameliorates this burden on SEFs. Any regulatory demand that SEFs set or monitor limits or levels is an impossible exercise that adds extraordinary costs.

4. Emergency authority

SEF Core Principle 8 requires a SEF to "adopt rules to provide for the exercise of emergency authority ... including the authority to liquidate or transfer open positions in

---

[183] CEA section 5h(f)(6); 7 U.S.C. 7b-3(f)(6).

any swap ...."[184] In its current form, this futures-based core principle places an impossible burden on SEFs. Congress should revise it to better suit the realities of the swaps market.

A SEF does not have the ability to liquidate or transfer open swaps positions because SEFs do not hold positions on behalf of their participants. As several commenters to the final SEF rules have explained, a SEF is not the appropriate entity to order the liquidation or transfer of these positions in an emergency because it does not have the ability or legal right to do so.[185] The Commission or a derivatives clearing organization (DCO), for cleared swaps, for example, are more appropriate entities to exercise this authority. Until Congress revises this futures-based core principle, the Commission and its staff should work to revise its guidance under SEF Core Principle 8 at most to require a SEF to adopt rules for coordination with a DCO or the CFTC to facilitate the liquidation or transfer of open positions in an emergency.[186]

5. Financial resources

SEF Core Principle 13 requires a SEF to have "financial resources [in an amount that] exceeds the total amount that would enable the [SEF] to cover the operating costs of the [SEF] for a 1-year period, as calculated on a rolling basis."[187]

The market impact of a SEF failure is not nearly comparable to a DCM failure so it does not make sense for a SEF to hold one year of financial resources. A SEF failure will not likely create a liquidity crisis because most swaps trade on multiple SEFs and thus there are multiple liquidity pools available in which to trade. Participants can easily trade on another SEF in the event of a failure. This is in contrast with the futures market where the impact on market liquidity is of greater concern in the event of a DCM failure because a DCM owns its products and those products only trade on the specific DCM. Thus, there is one liquidity pool. The failure of one DCM will likely harm this liquidity absent regulatory action to transfer those products and corresponding open interest to

---

[184] CEA section 5h(f)(8); 7 U.S.C. 7b-3(f)(8).
[185] SEF Rule at 33,536.
[186] Id.
[187] CEA section 5h(f)(13); 7 U.S.C. 7b-3(f)(13).

another DCM or participants moving to another product on another DCM. Given these differences, SEFs should not be held to the same one-year financial resources requirement as DCMs.

The financial resources requirement is overly burdensome and disproportionately impacts SEFs that offer voice-based execution methods. These SEFs must significantly increase their financial resources to cover the compensation of employee brokers who facilitate execution through these voice-based methods.[188] This requirement ties up additional capital for these SEFs, which puts them at a competitive disadvantage.

Congress should reexamine this core principle and only require a SEF to hold enough capital to conduct an orderly wind-down of its operations. It would not take a SEF one year to terminate employees and contracts and conduct an orderly wind-down of its operations. It would not be unreasonable to expect a SEF to conduct such a wind-down in three months.[189] This approach would release significant capital back to the SEF for innovation, lower barriers to entry, reduce costs and increase competition.

In the meantime, the Commission and staff should reexamine CFTC rules and work with SEFs to reduce their financial burden. The Commission and staff could, for example (a) flexibly interpret a SEF's financial resources to include additional resources such as projected revenues or projected capital contributions, (b) flexibly interpret operating costs to mean wind-down costs or to exclude certain costs not directly tied to core principle compliance or (c) flexibly interpret operating costs to exclude compensation that is not payable unless and until collected by the SEF.

---

[188] It is a common practice in traditional voice brokerage firms for the bulk of compensation of client-facing personnel to be calculated as a percentage of transaction commissions generated and collected by the employer. Such aggregate compensation is often one of the largest components of operating costs at such firms.
[189] *See, e.g.,* CME Comment Letter to SEF Rule, Appendix A, at 37 (Mar. 8, 2011), *available at* http://comments.cftc.gov/PublicComments/ViewComment.aspx?id=31276&SearchText=CME (stating that three months is an appropriate time frame for winding-down operations).

IV. ADVERSE CONSEQUENCES OF THE CFTC's SWAPS TRADING REGULATORY FRAMEWORK

Given the mismatch between the CFTC's flawed swaps trading regulatory framework and the manner in which swaps trade in global markets, the CFTC's swaps trading rules are causing numerous adverse consequences for U.S. market participants.

A. Global Market Fragmentation and Systemic Risk

Foremost among the adverse consequences is the reluctance of global market participants to transact with entities subject to CFTC swaps regulation. Traditionally, users of swaps products chose to do business with global financial institutions based on factors such as quality of service, product expertise, financial resources and professional relationship. Now, those criteria are secondary to the question of the institution's regulatory profile. Non-U.S. persons are avoiding financial firms bearing the scarlet letters of "U.S. person" in certain swaps products to steer clear of the CFTC's problematic regulations.[190] And it is not just American banks that are losing business, but also U.S. trading firms, intermediaries and asset managers, as well as the jobs of U.S.-based employees and vendors who support them.[191]

---

[190] *See* Audrey Costabile Blater, *Revisiting Cross-Border Fragmentation of Global OTC Derivatives: Mid-year 2014 Update,* ISDA Research Note, at 1-5 (Jul. 24, 2014), (ISDA Update), *available at* http://www2.isda.org/functional-areas/research/research-notes/ ("Following the October 2, 2013 SEF rule coming into force . . . relationships appear to have shifted as European dealers became reluctant to trade with US counterparties."); Philip Stafford, *CFTC Calls for International Help on Derivatives Oversight,* Financial Times, Nov. 14, 2014, *available at* http://www.ft.com/intl/cms/s/0/3aeabbb0-6b63-11e4-9337-00144feabdc0.html#axzz3OX6k3roi (indicating that because of recent CFTC regulations, "Sefs have become US-centric venues[, which] has led to concern that the market is fragmenting, damaging both economic growth and contributing to potential systemic market risk"); Philip Stafford, *US Swaps Trading Rules Have "Split Market,"* Financial Times, Jan. 21, 2014, *available at* http://www.ft.com/intl/cms/s/0/58251f84-82b8-11e3-8119-00144feab7de.html#axzz3CHQbMKxU (noting that "European dealers [have become] unwilling to trade with US counterparts" due to CFTC regulations) (Stafford, Market Split); Katy Burne, *Big U.S. Banks Make Swaps a Foreign Affair,* Wall Street Journal, Apr. 27, 2014, *available at* http://www.wsj.com/articles/SB10001424052702304788404579520302570888332?autologin=y (noting that some banks are "changing the terms of some swap agreements made by their offshore units so they don't get caught by U.S. regulations").

[191] The CFTC's swaps rules have even stymied overseas development of global electronic trading platforms in favor of traditional phone transactions that allow participants to readily identify a counterparty's now essential U.S./non-U.S. regulatory profile.

This avoidance by non-U.S. person market participants of the CFTC's ill-designed U.S. swaps trading rules is fragmenting global swaps markets between U.S. persons and non-U.S. persons and driving away global capital. Global swaps markets have divided into separate liquidity pools: those in which U.S. persons are able to participate and those in which U.S. persons are shunned. Liquidity has been fractured between an on-SEF, U.S. person market on one side, and an off-SEF, non-U.S. person market on the other.

According to a survey conducted by ISDA, the market for euro IRS has effectively split over the past 12 months.[192] Volumes between European and U.S. dealers have declined 77 percent since the introduction of the U.S. SEF regime.[193] The average cross-border volume of euro IRS transacted between European and U.S. dealers as a percentage of total euro IRS volume was 25 percent before the CFTC put its SEF regime in place, and has fallen to just 9 percent since.[194] According to an unnamed senior SEF executive, "The exit of the US banks has shifted trading in euro, yen and sterling interest rate swaps to Europe. Given that interest rate swaps are 80% of the overall [swaps] market, that's effectively half the swap market gone at a stroke."[195]

---

[192] *See* ISDA Update. *See also* Stafford, Market Split. Beginning on October 2, 2013 after the SEF rules compliance date, European dealers began to trade exclusively with other European counterparties in the market for euro interest rate swaps (IRS) and had dramatically moved away from trading with U.S. counterparties. ISDA Update at 4. In October 2013, 91 percent of euro IRS trades were between two European counterparties while only 9 percent were between a U.S. and a European dealer. *Id.* at 4-5. By May 2014, 93 percent of euro IRS trades were between two European counterparties while only 6 percent of euro IRS trades were between a U.S. and European dealer. *Id.* Compare these figures to those from a month before the SEF rules compliance date, when 71 percent of euro IRS trades were between two European counterparties while 29 percent of euro IRS trades were between a U.S. and European dealer. *Id.* European dealers have clearly shifted their trading behavior. This observation is also supported by an ISDA survey where 68 percent of non-U.S. market participant respondents indicated they have reduced or ceased trading with U.S. persons. Audrey Costabile Blater, *Footnote 88 and Market Fragmentation: An ISDA Survey*, ISDA Research Note, at 3-4 (Dec. 18, 2013), *available at* http://www2.isda.org/functional-areas/research/research-notes/.
[193] ISDA Update at 6.
[194] *Id* at 2. *See also* Amir Khwaja, *A Review of 2014 US Swap Volumes and SEF Market Share*, TABB Forum (Jan. 16, 2015), *available at* http://tabbforum.com/opinions/a-review-of-2014-us-swap-volumes-and-sef-market-share (noting that the majority of trading in EUR, JPY and GBP IRS is taking place off-SEF in Europe, Japan and London).
[195] Kim Hunter, *Growing Pains*, Markit Magazine, at 32 (Winter 2014), *available at* http://content.markitcdn.com/corporate/Company/Files/MagazineEntireIssue?CMSID=1277525de02549a dbf7b422b9b34f641 (Hunter).

The fragmentation of the global swaps market has fractured trading liquidity, exacerbating the inherent challenge of swaps trading – adequate liquidity.[196] Fragmentation has led to smaller, disconnected liquidity pools and less efficient and more volatile pricing. Divided markets are more brittle, with shallower liquidity, posing a risk of failure in times of economic stress or crisis. Fragmentation also increases firms' operational risks as they structure themselves to avoid U.S. rules and now must manage multiple liquidity pools in different jurisdictions (e.g., through different affiliates). This activity increases a firm's operational and structural complexity and reduces its efficiency in the markets. In short, market fragmentation caused by the CFTC's ill-designed trading rules – and the application of those rules abroad – is harming liquidity, increasing the systemic risk that the Dodd-Frank Act was predicated on reducing, and driving capital overseas as non-U.S. persons seek to avoid the CFTC's swaps trading rules.

There are at least two underreported impacts of global market fragmentation. First, the emergence of separate U.S. person and non-U.S. person swaps liquidity pools increases the likelihood of different pricing in the divergent swaps markets.[197] Meanwhile, global regulators are keen to reform global indices such as the London Interbank Offered Rate (LIBOR) to use transaction-based data rather than indicative market data. However, the development of disparate pricing in two distinct trading markets will make attempts to unify benchmark calculations extraordinarily challenging. Second, as trading in non-U.S. person markets continues to grow at the expense of U.S. person markets, bank prudential regulators in London and Singapore are requiring supervised entities, including subsidiaries of U.S. banking institutions, to increase capital reserves to meet Basel III capital and liquidity requirements. For U.S. bank subsidiaries, these requirements may well be met through the exporting of capital from

---

[196] Referring to the manifest liquidity split between London and New York, Dexter Senft, Morgan Stanley's co-head of fixed income electronic markets, said, "I liken [SEF liquidity] to a canary in a coal mine. It's not dead yet, but it's lying on its side." *Id.* at 31. *See also* Katy Burne, *Companies Warn of Swaps Rules' Impact on Hedging*, Wall Street Journal, Apr. 8, 2014, *available at* http://www.wsj.com/articles/SB10001424052702304819004579489493056041978?autologin=y (noting fragmentation and liquidity concerns).

[197] Such a divergence in U.S. bank and non-U.S. bank lending rates took place during the height of the Eurodollar market.

the U.S. Simply put, the more swaps that are traded away from CFTC-regulated swaps markets, the more capital and liquidity that may flow away from the U.S. economy.

There are some who may argue that the fragmentation problem is simply one of regulatory arbitrage. They contend that trading will naturally flow away for some time from the U.S. to Europe and other jurisdictions that have yet to adopt swaps transaction-level rules. They argue that the Europeans and others are just taking too long to adopt transaction-level rules and that, once they do, the fragmentation of global swaps markets will reverse itself. To them the problem is just temporary.

This argument is far too forgiving of the CFTC's flawed rule set and ignores the resultant long-term harm to U.S. financial markets. The argument is built on the assumption that, if the Europeans and others could just be hurried along in their rule writing, they will adopt the same flawed rule set as the CFTC. Unfortunately, the Europeans are not looking to make the same mistakes.[198] It has been clear for a long time that European swaps trading rules will not narrowly limit methods of swaps execution nor impose many of the other peculiar CFTC trading restrictions described in this White Paper. The Europeans also do not appear willing to be hurried. They have been clear from the outset that the transaction-level swaps rules are tertiary in importance to trade reporting and clearing and will be addressed with that level of priority. The defense of current CFTC swaps trading rules further assumes that, once swaps markets leave the U.S., they can easily be brought back. Sadly, the history of trading markets, such as the Eurodollar market,[199] demonstrates that, even when

---

[198] Inevitably, European market regulators may make some unique mistakes of their own.

[199] Milton Friedman, *The Euro-Dollar Market, Some First Principles,* University of Chicago, Selected Papers No. 34, *available at* http://www.chicagobooth.edu/~/media/44CEE6C8A25B4FF2A48925163DAA2F85.pdf. Friedman makes the case that the development of the multi-trillion dollar Euro-dollar market was primarily the result of the Federal Reserve's Regulation Q in the 1970s, which fixed maximum interest rates that Fed member banks could pay on time deposits. As a result European (mostly London) banks paying higher interest rates became more attractive than U.S. deposits, and the Euro-dollar and later Asian-dollar markets expanded outside the U.S. Friedman also blames direct and indirect U.S. exchange controls imposed for "balance-of-payments" purposes. Despite the later withdrawal of Regulation Q and various exchange controls, the Euro and Asian Dollar markets remain firmly offshore where they continue to grow.

regulators address fundamental flaws, it is hard to bring departed markets back to U.S. shores along with the American jobs they once supported.[200]

B. Domestic Market Fragmentation

In addition to global swaps market fragmentation, the CFTC's unwarranted slicing and dicing of swaps trading into a series of novel regulatory categories, such as Required Transactions and Permitted Transactions and block transactions "off-SEF" and non-blocks "on-SEF," each with their corresponding execution methods, has fragmented the U.S. swaps market into artificial market segments. This fragmentation comes on top of the already inevitable segmentation caused by distinct SEC swaps transaction rules for securities-based swaps.[201] This fragmentation has exacerbated the inherent challenge of adequate trading liquidity. Like global fragmentation, domestic fragmentation has led to an artificial series of smaller and smaller pools of trading liquidity and an increase in market inefficiencies. So long as such disparate segments remain, U.S. swaps markets face a self-imposed liquidity challenge as compared with non-U.S. markets.

C. Market Liquidity Risk

A 2013 staff report from the New York Fed asks whether the reduced liquidity-provision capacity of dealers, as a result of the Volcker Rule and other new capital constraints, will encourage greater market making by non-dealer institutional investors to fill the void and result in a more stable financial system.[202] The report analyzes the liquidity-making activities of major sell-side dealers in corporate bond and CDS markets during the 2008 financial crisis.[203] It concludes that during the height of the crisis, sell-side dealers generally performed their customary role as liquidity makers when their clients demanded liquidity.[204] But the authors explain that, despite this dealer-provided

---

[200] *Id.*
[201] As of this White Paper's publication date, the SEC has not promulgated final security-based SEF rules.
[202] Jaewon Choi and Or Shachar, *Did Liquidity Providers Become Liquidity Seekers?*, Federal Reserve Bank of New York, Staff Report No. 650 (Oct. 2013), *available at* http://www.newyorkfed.org/research/staff_reports/sr650.pdf (Choi and Shachar).
[203] *Id.*
[204] *Id.* at 17.

liquidity, there was still a shortfall in corporate bond liquidity driving a large negative CDS-bond basis.[205] The authors hypothesize that the bulk of liquidity taking during this period was driven by highly-levered traders and hedge funds.[206] The report expresses doubt on the desirability of offsetting sell-side dealers' traditional market-making capacity with liquidity from non-dealer institutional investors, including arbitrageurs.[207]

A more recent report by the Office of Financial Research of the U.S. Treasury Department makes clear that changes in financial market structures caused by new regulations will reduce the willingness of some major market participants to smooth out volatility in global financial markets.[208] According to this study, these changes will cause the U.S. financial system to become more vulnerable to debilitating financial market shocks.[209]

Market analyst Anthony Perrotta has explained how the October 15, 2014 crash in the U.S. Treasury market was fundamentally driven by structural imbalance in the ratio of liquidity provided to markets and liquidity demanded from markets.[210] He explains:

> Under the current, principal-based risk model, liquidity providers – traditionally large banks with significant amounts of capital – provide liquidity on-demand (a.k.a. "immediacy") to investors. As the amount of capital these banks have at their disposal and committed to market-making declines due to regulations imposed by the Dodd-Frank Act and Basel III Accords – including the Volcker Rule and the liquidity coverage ratio (LCR) – the likelihood of volatility increasing is greater ... and the amount of on-demand liquidity requested can sometimes overwhelm the liquidity providing universe."[211]

---

[205] *Id.* at 18-22.
[206] *Id.* at 19.
[207] *Id.* at 22-23.
[208] *2014 Annual Report*, Office of Financial Research, U.S. Treasury Department, at 30-33 (Dec. 2, 2014), *available at* http://www.treasury.gov/initiatives/ofr/about/Documents/OFR_AnnualReport2014_FINAL_12-1-2014.pdf.
[209] *Id.*
[210] Perrotta.
[211] *Id.*

In light of these government studies and industry observations about liquidity shortfall in corporate and U.S. government debt markets, there is good reason for concern that CFTC regulations and staff actions may be hazarding a similar structural imbalance between liquidity provided and liquidity demanded in the U.S. swaps markets. The CFTC's restrictions on methods of execution and its slicing and dicing of regulatory categories are a challenge to broad liquidity formation both cross-border and domestically. The CFTC's embargo rule is inhibiting the established role of "work-up" in fostering greater trading liquidity. Its void *ab initio* policy increases risk of failed execution, inhibiting transaction volume. Misinterpretation of the impartial access requirement to hasten the emergence of all-to-all swaps markets may hamper sell-side dealers' access to D2D marketplaces to hedge swaps inventory. Without ready access to D2D markets, sell-side dealers may withdraw from the market or charge their buy-side customers much higher prices. This could leave buy-side customers with volatile pricing and without sufficient liquidity, especially during periods of volatility, when they need it most.

D. Threaten SEF Survival

The CFTC's swaps trading regime threatens the survival of many SEFs and has erected enormous barriers to entry for future registrants. The CFTC's prescriptive and burdensome rules have ensured that operating a SEF is an expensive, legally intensive activity.[212] The CFTC staff has unnecessarily added to this burden by issuing an unprecedented number of no-action letters, guidance, advisories, and other written communications.[213] On the revenue side, the mismatch between the CFTC's swaps trading framework and the natural commercial workings of the swaps market has caused participants to avoid the CFTC's SEF regime, sharply depressing revenues.[214] According to one SEF executive, "Some of those [SEFs] with volume are not making a

---

[212] Catherine Contiguglia, *Sef Boss Spends His Days 'Worrying About Costs,'* Risk.net, Sep. 24, 2014, *available at* http://www.risk.net/risk-magazine/news/2371788/sef-boss-spends-his-days-worrying-about-costs (Contiguglia).

[213] *See* Hester Peirce, *Regulating through the Back Door at the Commodity Futures Trading Commission,* Mercatus Working Paper (Nov. 2014), *available at* http://mercatus.org/sites/default/files/Peirce-Back-Door-CFTC.pdf (detailing how the CFTC used non-rulemaking methods to impose binding obligations on regulated persons).

[214] Contiguglia.

profit; the rest must be wondering how they can keep the lights on."[215] As a result, the CFTC has guaranteed that large, well-resourced corporations that operate SEFs have an advantage over smaller platforms. As the head of Ice Swap Trade recently stated, "it has become clear [that operating a SEF] ... is never going to be a standalone business."[216] Without change, the CFTC's current swaps trading regime is ensuring that big platforms get bigger, small platforms get squeezed out and operating a SEF is unprofitable. The Dodd-Frank Act did not authorize a regulatory drive for SEF consolidation.

E. Hinder Technological Innovation

In 1899, U.S. Patent Commissioner Charles H. Duell is said to have pronounced that "everything that can be invented has been invented."[217] Not to be outdone, the CFTC's swaps trading rules pre-suppose that order book and RFQ methodologies are today and will always remain the only suitable technological means for U.S. swaps execution. These restrictive SEF rules would close U.S. swaps markets to promising technological advances while the rest of the world proceeds ahead in financial market innovation.[218]

A particular example is Dutch Auction-based electronic trading systems, which are actively deployed in swaps markets around the world. These systems generally deploy algorithms based on time priority that match participants' orders at pre-determined prices, while protecting participant trading intentions as to side of market and size.[219] They have the ability to electronically concentrate otherwise elusive liquidity in episodically traded markets by bringing participants together and enabling them to execute orders based on a single pre-determined market clearing price without the

---

[215] Hunter at 32.

[216] *Id.*

[217] Charles Holland Duell, Wikipedia, *available at* http://en.wikipedia.org/wiki/Charles_Holland_Duell. The statement has been debunked as apocryphal.

[218] *See* Section III.A. (discussing a SEF's limited execution methods).

[219] Definition of Dutch Auction, Investopedia, *available at* http://www.investopedia.com/terms/d/dutchauction.asp. *See also* BGC Derivatives Markets, L.P. SEF Rules, Rule 602(c) and (d), Volume Match Trading Facility and Volume Match Plus Trading Facility, *available at* http://www.bgcsef.com/BGC_SEF_Rulebook_11_01_13_Clean.pdf.

adverse price effects resulting from large-sized orders. Thus, Dutch Auction trading protocols promote liquidity and price transparency in these markets with episodic liquidity in a way CLOBs cannot. Participants may also obtain a better price through a Dutch Auction as compared with a CLOB given that there may be few bids and offers in the CLOB in illiquid markets or after periods of illiquidity.

Unfortunately, the CFTC's limited methods of SEF execution and CFTC staff's interpretation of those methods may prohibit these valuable auction-based electronic trading platforms, notwithstanding Congress's clear permission for "any means of interstate commerce."[220] This prohibition would be especially unjustifiable given that Dutch Auctions use a method similar to DCMs' currently permitted process for the daily opening of electronically traded futures markets.[221] For example, CME Rule 573 establishes procedures for the Globex opening with a single equilibrium opening price.[222] Globex determines this equilibrium price based on sell pressure and buy pressure where the largest volume of trading can occur.[223] There has been no suggestion that this process does not comport with the statutory definition of a trading facility, which DCMs are required to offer.[224] Therefore, any effort to prohibit Dutch Auctions appears contrary to CFTC regulations and precedent, let alone the expressed flexibility of Title VII of the Dodd-Frank Act.

F. Introduce High-Frequency Trading

In an odd twist, the CFTC's insistence upon RFQ systems and centralized, order-driven markets to execute swaps transactions has the potential to open U.S. swaps markets to algorithmic trading and HFT. While the HFT debate is beyond the scope of this paper, the CFTC's unwarranted bias for certain execution methods raises important public policy concerns regarding algorithmic trading and HFT. It is unclear how those who support the CFTC's impetus for electronic CLOB execution of swaps, yet decry

---

[220] CEA section 1a(50); 7 U.S.C. 1a(50).
[221] *See, e.g.,* CME Rule 573, Globex Opening, *available at* http://www.cmegroup.com/rulebook/CME/I/5/5.pdf.
[222] *Id.*
[223] *Id.*
[224] CEA section 1a(51); 7 U.S.C. 1a(51).

HFT in today's equities and futures markets, will reconcile these views when the enormous but humanly-managed swaps markets are launched into unmanned hyperspace by HFT algorithmic trading technologies.

G. <u>Waste Taxpayer Dollars</u>

Managing the CFTC's flawed swaps trading regulatory framework is expensive and time consuming. Fitting the square peg of the CFTC's swaps trading rules into the round hole of the established global swaps markets requires the Commission and staff to devote enormous resources to continuously explain, clarify, adjust, exempt and manipulate rules sufficient for rough swaps market operability. The Commission and staff must constantly add to the plethora of no-action letters, guidance, staff advisories and other written communications that go out to the market and participants. During the course of implementing the Dodd-Frank Act, the Commission staff has issued 334 such communications.[225] The package transactions example discussed earlier is a clear instance of the large amounts of staff resources expended. This mismatch is also requiring the CFTC and its staff to expend considerable resources on issues that would not be issues if the rules followed congressional intent and aligned with swaps market dynamics. The NDF clearing mandate debate discussed earlier is another example. The CFTC's current swaps trading regulatory framework requires enormous bureaucratic "make work" to assure industry compliance. Yet, it is mostly unnecessary and unsupported by Title VII of the Dodd-Frank Act. It wastes taxpayer dollars at a time when the Commission is seeking additional resources from Congress.

H. <u>Harm Relations with Foreign Regulators</u>

At the 2009 Pittsburgh G-20 Summit, one year after the financial crisis, global leaders agreed to work together to support economic recovery through a "Framework for Strong, Sustainable and Balanced Growth."[226] The Pittsburgh participants pledged to

---

[225] As of Jan. 13, 2015, the Commission staff has issued 250 no-action letters, 42 exemptive letters and 42 staff interpretive letters, guidance, advisories and other written communications.
[226] G-20 Leaders' Statement, The Pittsburgh Summit, at 2 (Sep. 24-25, 2009), *available at* https://www.g20.org/sites/default/files/g20_resources/library/Pittsburgh_Declaration.pdf.

work together to "implement global standards" in financial markets, while rejecting "protectionism."[227]

Instead of working with its counterparts abroad, the CFTC forged ahead with overreaching swaps rules, which are partially responsible for harming relations with foreign regulators. The CFTC exported its swaps rules overseas through its July 2013 "Interpretive Guidance and Policy Statement Regarding Compliance With Certain Swap Regulations" (Interpretive Guidance).[228] In essence, the Interpretive Guidance asserted that every single swap a U.S. person enters into, no matter where it is transacted, has a direct and significant connection with activities in, and effect on, commerce of the United States that requires imposing CFTC transaction rules.[229]

Several months later, the CFTC staff issued a "Staff Advisory" that declared that, even if no U.S. person is a party to the trade, CFTC transaction rules apply if it is "arranged, negotiated, or executed" by personnel or agents of a non-U.S. swap dealer located in the U.S.[230] If that was not enough, staff issued guidance the next day stating that it "expects that a multilateral swaps trading platform located outside the United States that provides U.S. persons or persons located in the U.S. (including personnel and agents of non-U.S. persons located in the United States) ... with the ability to trade or execute swaps on or pursuant to the rules of the platform, either directly or indirectly through an intermediary, will register as a SEF or DCM."[231]

Taken together, the combined effect of the CFTC's Interpretive Guidance, Staff Advisory and staff guidance – none of which is a formally adopted CFTC rule – is to dictate that non-U.S. market operators and participants must abide by flawed swaps transaction-level rules for trades involving U.S. persons or supported by U.S.-based

---

[227] *Id.* at 7.
[228] Interpretive Guidance and Policy Statement Regarding Compliance With Certain Swap Regulations, 78 FR 45,292 (Jul. 26, 2013).
[229] *Id.*
[230] CFTC Staff Advisory No. 13-69, *Applicability of Transaction-Level Requirements to Activity in the United States* (Nov. 14, 2013), *available at* http://www.cftc.gov/ucm/groups/public/@lrlettergeneral/documents/letter/13-69.pdf.
[231] Division of Market Oversight Guidance on Application of Certain Commission Regulations to Swap Execution Facilities, at 2 (Nov. 15, 2013), *available at* http://www.cftc.gov/ucm/groups/public/@newsroom/documents/file/dmosefguidance111513.pdf.

personnel. This approach flew in the face of harmonization efforts, such as the CFTC-European Union Path Forward understanding.[232] The CFTC's relationship with foreign regulators and global swaps market participants has been strained as a result of the CFTC's global overreach.[233]

I. **Threaten Job Creation and Human Discretion**

The application of certain CFTC rules threatens jobs in the U.S. financial services industry. As explained in Section IV.H., the CFTC's Staff Advisory imposed swaps transaction rules on trades between non-U.S. persons whenever anyone on U.S. soil "arranged, negotiated, or executed" the trade.[234] While the Staff Advisory was recently delayed for the fourth time, it is causing many overseas trading firms to consider cutting off all activity with U.S.-based trade support personnel to avoid subjecting themselves to the CFTC's flawed swaps trading rules.[235] The Staff Advisory jeopardizes the role of bank sales personnel in U.S. financial centers like Boston, Charlotte, Chicago, New Jersey and New York. It will likely have a ripple effect on technology staff supporting U.S. electronic trading systems, along with the thousands of jobs tied to the vendors who provide food services, office support, custodial services and transportation needs to the U.S. financial services industry. With tens of millions of Americans falling back on part-time work, the CFTC should not cause good-paying full-time jobs to be eliminated.[236]

---

[232] Cross-Border Regulation of Swaps/Derivatives Discussions between the Commodity Futures Trading Commission and the European Union – A Path Forward, Jul. 11, 2013, *available at* http://www.cftc.gov/PressRoom/PressReleases/pr6640-13.

[233] *See, e.g.,* Andrew Ackerman et al., *U.S., Europe Hit Impasse Over Rules on Derivatives*, Wall Street Journal, Sep. 25, 2014, *available at* http://online.wsj.com/articles/u-s-europe-hit-impasse-over-rules-on-derivatives-1411672215; Gina Chon and Michael MacKenzie, *CFTC Leadership Change Eases Strains*, Financial Times, Feb. 13, 2014, *available at* http://www.ft.com/intl/cms/s/0/3149635c-9401-11e3-bf0c-00144feab7de.html#axzz3LuyOpxFA. *See also* J. Christopher Giancarlo, Commissioner, Keynote Address of CFTC Commissioner J. Christopher Giancarlo at The Global Forum for Derivatives Markets, 35th Annual Burgenstock Conference, Geneva, Switzerland: The Looming Cross-Atlantic Derivatives Trade War: "A Return to Smoot-Hawley" (Sep. 24, 2014), *available at* http://www.cftc.gov/PressRoom/SpeechesTestimony/opagiancarlos-1.

[234] CFTC Staff Advisory No. 13-69.

[235] CFTC Letter No. 14-140, *Extension of No-Action Relief: Transaction-Level Requirements for Non-U.S. Swap Dealers* (Nov. 14, 2014), *available at* http://www.cftc.gov/ucm/groups/public/@lrlettergeneral/documents/letter/14-140.pdf.

[236] News Release, *The Employment Situation – September 2014*, Bureau of Labor Statistics, at Summary Table A, Oct. 3, 2014, *available at* http://www.bls.gov/news.release/archives/empsit_10032014.pdf. Steve

It is apparent to observers that underlying many CFTC rules and regulations is an unstated bias against human discretion in swaps execution.[237] The bias is seen in a range of CFTC positions, including allowing only two specific types of execution methods for Required Transactions,[238] requiring an RFQ System to operate in conjunction with an Order Book,[239] requiring an RFQ to be sent to three market participants,[240] placing various conditions around basis risk mitigation services[241] and the CFTC staff's aversion to Dutch Auctions that utilize professional discretion in setting opening auction prices.[242] Yet, there is no legal support in Title VII of Dodd-Frank for restricting human discretion in swaps execution.

Indeed, the CFTC's bias against human discretion is contrary to what is transpiring in the U.S.'s most successful financial marketplace. The two major markets for initial public offerings (IPOs), Nasdaq and the New York Stock Exchange (NYSE), are today competing against one another on the basis of which has the better degree of "human touch" in the IPO process.[243] These markets tout the role of professional discretion in determining a range of trading factors, including opening price, when trading begins and "price parameters to limit movements in the last few seconds before the open."[244] The human element is now seen as a key safeguard against the type of runaway technical errors that plagued Facebook's 2012 IPO, when "more than 30,000

Moore, *Under Obama: One Million More Americans Have Dropped Out Of Work Force than Have Found a Job*, Forbes, Oct. 6, 2014, *available at* http://www.forbes.com/sites/stevemoore/2014/10/06/under-obama-one-million-more-americans-have-dropped-out-of-work-force-than-have-found-a-job/.

[237] Regulatory pressure will force trading innovation to be "driven by the need for new mechanisms to ensure staff and clients don't misbehave," *See* Larry Tabb, *Peering Into the Future – Yelling and Screaming in 2015, But Little Radical Change*, Tabb Forum, Jan. 2, 2015, *available at* http://tabbforum.com/opinions/peering-into-the-future-yelling-and-screaming-in-2015-but-little-radical-change.

[238] 17 C.F.R. 37.9(a)(2).

[239] *Id.* and 17. C.F.R. 37.9(a)(3).

[240] 17 C.F.R. 37.9(a)(3).

[241] *See* Section V.C.4.

[242] *See* Section V.D.

[243] Sam Mamudi, *Nasdaq Tries Human Beings to Stave Off IPO Poaching by Bid Board*, Bloomberg, Jan. 6, 2015, *available at* http://www.bloomberg.com/news/2015-01-06/nasdaq-highlights-human-touch-in-ipo-process-to-fend-off-nyse.html.

[244] *Id.*

buy and sell orders were either canceled or delayed, leading to a $10 million fine from the U.S. Securities and Exchange Commission."[245]

There is no ascertainable policy purpose in promoting human discretion in equity public offerings while restricting it in U.S. swaps trading. It would be a regulatory failure to restrict human discretion in the $600 trillion swaps markets, and herd trading onto automated electronic platforms, where software failures and other technical glitches could someday cause a "flash crash" unlike anything yet seen in global markets.

J. Increase Market Fragility

Nassim Nicholas Taleb, the well-known options trader who coined the phrase "Black Swan," has written about the increased fragility of today's top-down designed, overly complicated economic systems.[246] He warns that naïve over-intervention in complex systems such as financial markets make them more vulnerable, not less, to cascading runaway chains of reactions and ultimately fragile in the face of outsized crisis events.[247] He posits that the opposite of such fragility is not more robust or durable systems, but systems that are "anti-fragile."[248] Taleb uses "anti-fragile" to mean systems that become stronger when subject to stress, the way a human body becomes immune to a disease through inoculation.[249] Taleb explains that financial markets that are allowed to grow organically through trial and error and gain and loss, with plenty of redundancy, cyclical stresses and disorders, best resemble biological organisms that adapt and, indeed, thrive, in the face of shock and partial destruction.[250] He also explains how systems artificially directed through untested regulatory prescriptions intended to limit randomness and avoid systemic stress become increasingly prone to fail in the face of sudden shocks.[251]

---

[245] Id.

[246] See generally Nassim Nicholas Taleb, Antifragile: Things That Gain From Disorder (Random House 2012).

[247] Id.

[248] Id.

[249] Id.

[250] Id.

[251] Id.

Unfortunately, the CFTC swaps trading rules, with their prescriptive complexity, limits on human discretion and transaction methodology bias, seem to support this type of systemic fragility. That fragility increases rather than decreases the systemic risk – the risk of failure of the swaps markets and the broader U.S. financial system – that the Dodd-Frank Act was ostensibly designed to reduce. Instead, the CFTC's rules should allow for the supervised but natural development of U.S. swaps markets with all the richness and redundancy such organic development entails and the benefits of U.S. economic health and prosperity that "anti-fragility" can provide.

V. ALTERNATIVE SWAPS TRADING REGULATORY FRAMEWORK

This White Paper proposes a pro-reform reconsideration of many of the CFTC's swaps trading rules to align with natural swaps market dynamics and the express statutory framework of Title VII of the Dodd-Frank Act. This reconsideration of the swaps trading rules is drawn from five key tenets: comprehensiveness, cohesiveness, flexibility, professionalism and transparency. This section provides a high-level overview of this alternative swaps trading regulatory framework focusing on these five key tenets.

A. Comprehensiveness

The first tenet of this White Paper's alternative framework is to subject a comprehensive range of U.S. swaps trading activity to CFTC oversight. In this respect, the CFTC implemented a broad SEF registration requirement.[252] The final SEF rules explain that registration applies "to facilities that meet the SEF definition in CEA section 1a(50)."[253] This White Paper supports that comprehensive approach.

As the CFTC noted in the final SEF rules, the Dodd-Frank Act contains some ambiguity regarding SEF registration.[254] Given this ambiguity, some market participants have argued that Congress did not intend to require CFTC registration for platforms that meet the SEF definition, but only facilitate swaps not subject to the trade execution requirement.[255] However, the CFTC has already required SEF registration for any platform that meets the SEF definition, even if it only facilitates swaps not subject to the trade execution requirement.[256] Such SEF platforms are already temporarily registered.[257]

Furthermore, Congress generally intended in Title VII to bring all facilities for swaps trading into a comprehensive regulatory structure, not just a portion, through its

---

[252] 17 C.F.R. 37.3(a)(1); SEF Rule at 33,481-483.
[253] SEF Rule at 33,481.
[254] *See* SEF Rule at 33,481-482.
[255] *See* SEF Rule at 33,479-480.
[256] *See* SEF Rule at 33,481 n. 88.
[257] As of Jan. 13, 2015, the Commission has temporarily registered 22 SEFs. *See* CFTC website, http://sirt.cftc.gov/SIRT/SIRT.aspx?Topic=SwapExecutionFacilities.

broad SEF registration provision.[258] Leaving platforms that solely facilitate the execution of swaps not subject to the trade execution mandate outside of CFTC oversight, and those that facilitate swaps subject to the mandate within, as some commenters have suggested, creates bifurcated regulated and unregulated markets and invites abuses and evasion.[259]

This White Paper proposes to adopt the CFTC's registration approach, albeit in a clear and direct manner. The scope of SEF registration should be defined through rules and not buried footnotes in the preamble text, such as the widely consequential impact of the CFTC's now famous footnote 88.[260] Similarly, this White Paper proposes that all key components of the CFTC's swaps rules reside in clear and definitive rule text and not in footnotes, staff advisories and ad-hoc no-action letters.

B. Cohesiveness

The second tenet of this White Paper's alternative framework is regulatory cohesiveness. This approach would remove the artificial segmentation between Required Transactions and their limited execution methods and Permitted Transactions and their broad execution methods, and between block transactions "off-SEF" and non-blocks "on-SEF." There is no statutory support for these divisions. They carry no ostensible policy justification. They are at odds with accepted global practices of swaps trading and hinder liquidity formation.[261] They add large and unjustifiable regulatory costs and burdens and absorb limited agency resources. Instead, all CFTC-regulated swaps trading should fall within the same, cohesive and undivided regulatory framework.

---

[258] The SEF registration requirement states "[n]o person may operate a facility for the trading or processing of swaps unless the facility is registered as a [SEF] or as a [DCM] under this section." CEA section 5h(a)(1); 7 U.S.C. 7b-3(a)(1).
[259] *E.g.,* A platform meeting the SEF definition could shift its offerings to eliminate swaps imminently subject to a trade execution mandate in order to stay outside of CFTC oversight.
[260] *See* SEF Rule at 33,481 n. 88.
[261] *See* Section IV.B. and C. (discussing fragmentation and market liquidity risk).

C. Flexibility

This straightforward, comprehensive and cohesive approach will only work, however, if the CFTC returns to the Dodd-Frank Act's express prescription for flexibility in swaps trading as outlined below. This White Paper proposes congressionally authorized flexibility in the following five key areas:

1. Permitting trade execution through "any means of interstate commerce"
2. Allowing products to evolve naturally
3. Letting market structure be determined by the market
4. Accommodating beneficial swaps market practices
5. Treating core principles as general principles

1. Permit trade execution through "any means of interstate commerce"

This White Paper proposes that U.S. swaps markets be reopened to business and technological innovation that is currently stymied by CFTC swaps trading rules. Technology is improving American lives today in many ways, from hailing a taxi (*e.g.,* Uber) and connecting with business colleagues (*e.g.,* Linkedin) to listening to music (*e.g.,* Spotify). Technological innovations are also transforming capital markets in areas such as raising money for business start-ups (*e.g.,* Kickstarter) and consumer borrowing (*e.g.,* Payoff). These innovations lower barriers to entry, reduce costs and open markets to a broader range of participants. Unfortunately, the CFTC's swaps rules would prevent such technological innovation in the U.S. swaps markets.

Prudent regulatory oversight should allow methods of swaps execution to evolve organically based on technological innovation, customer demand and quality of service. SEFs, not regulators, should decide what methods of swaps execution are most suitable for the instruments they seek to execute and most useful to the particular customers they choose to serve. SEFs, not regulators, should decide in which promising new business methods and technologies to invest or not to invest. Similarly, market participants must not be denied the flexibility to choose what execution method is best suited to their swaps trading and liquidity needs. Therefore, the swaps market should continue to allow its participants a broad choice of methods of swaps execution, including, but not limited to, electronic CLOBs, simple order books, RFQ systems, electronic Dutch Auctions, hybrid electronic and voice execution methods, full voice-based execution methods, work-up and any other "means of interstate commerce" that may today or in the future satisfy customer swaps trading and liquidity requirements. Markets, not regulators, must determine the various means of interstate commerce utilized in the swaps market. That is clearly what Congress intended.

2. Allow products to evolve naturally

This White Paper proposes a more commonsense approach to mandatory product trading on SEFs. That is, let new and novel swaps products develop commercially to the point where market participants naturally turn to platforms to offer trading in the product. Once that happens, the product must trade on a DCM or registered SEF. This evolution reflects the reality in the global swaps markets that participants initially trade newly developed swaps products bilaterally and only move to third-party trading platforms once commercial trading reaches a critical stage.

The Dodd-Frank Act trade execution requirement expresses this logic in that a clearing mandated swap must be executed on a SEF unless no SEF makes that swap available to trade (*i.e.,* offers the swap for trading).[262] This White Paper proposes to follow this simple approach and do away with the MAT process. As explained in Section III.C., the MAT process is not supported by the statutory language and has no sound policy basis. Simply following congressional intent would save precious resources. Anything more complicated is just regulatory make-work.

3. Let market structure be determined by the market

This White Paper proposes a more flexible approach to swaps market structure. As an essential governing principle, governments and regulators should not pick winners and losers in the commercial economy. Regulators should not substitute their judgment for the business judgment of commercial entities and participants.

---

[262] CEA section 2(h)(8); 7 U.S.C. 2(h)(8).

This White Paper asserts that there is no "all-to-all" trading mandate set forth in Title VII of the Dodd-Frank Act and the Commission does not have the authority to impose one. Accordingly, this White Paper does not advocate for any particular market structure, such as existing separate D2D and D2C markets or combined all-to-all markets, but simply calls for letting participants in the marketplace determine the optimal market structure based on their swaps trading needs and objectives. Adhering to Congress's mandate for flexible methods of execution will allow for a more organic and customer-driven development of swaps market structure and the necessary balancing of liquidity demand and liquidity provision.

SEF platforms must have the right to offer their services to segments of the swaps markets that they believe they are best qualified to serve, so long as they do so on an impartial basis consistent with the statute. Similarly, swaps participants must have the right to impartial treatment in seeking to transact with whichever CFTC-registered platform they determine to provide the best service for their specific needs.

In a similar regard, SEFs should be free to operate either on a name give-up or anonymous basis as they deem appropriate in the interest of the clients they serve. Nevertheless, such freedom of choice should not prevent customer-driven approaches to post-trade disclosure, in which SEF participants could individually elect whether or not to permit limited identifying information to be provided to trade counterparties following a transaction.

4. Accommodate beneficial swaps market practices

This White Paper proposes to better accommodate established and beneficial swaps market practices. For example, the proposal would allow SEFs to implement clear, workable error trade policies to address the situation where an executed swaps transaction is rejected from clearing. It would also end the void *ab initio* policy that is not statutorily sound, creates a competitive disadvantage relative to the U.S. futures market and introduces unjustifiable risk to U.S. swaps transactions.

This proposal would also narrow the scope of confirmations for uncleared swaps to include only their primary and other material economic terms. There would be no need for confirmations to either supersede or reference master agreements or require SEFs to possess such agreements. It is practicably impossible for a SEF to collect and track changes to every agreement between participants, and to have to "glean" any information from these agreements for confirmation and reporting purposes.[263] If there is a concern that master or other agreements may be used to change the economic terms of a transaction entered into on a SEF, then SEF-issued confirmations could be structured to supersede the terms of any agreement between the counterparties that contradict transaction-specific economic terms in the confirmation.

This proposal would also better accommodate the activities of third-party commercial service providers, such as swaps trade data vendors, trade term affirmation providers and trade confirmation vendors. As explained in Section I.C., the swaps market has had a history of third-party service providers, unlike the futures market, where DCMs handle these functions. These differing approaches are the result of differences in product development. One approach is not necessarily better than the other, and the proposal would provide the appropriate flexibility to accommodate both regimes so that market participants can decide which approach they prefer.

Similarly, this proposal would also take a benign view of compression, risk reduction, risk recycling, dynamic hedging and other similar services that provide operational efficiencies and crucial systemic risk reduction. As explained in Section I.C., these services exist in the swaps market, as opposed to the futures market, given the non-standardized terms and conditions of swaps products that make it operationally challenging to offset risk. At its core, the Dodd-Frank Act was aimed at reducing systemic risk. These services support this objective by using technology and continual innovation to meet the market's risk-management needs. These activities should not be limited by forcing service providers to comply with misguided registration requirements

---

[263] CFTC Letter No. 14-108 at 4.

or with certain limited execution methods.[264] Any other approach would be contrary to the public good of systemic risk reduction.

5. Treat core principles as general principles

This White Paper proposes to treat the SEF core principles as true principles rather than rigid rule sets. First, the framework would revise many of the futures-based SEF core principles to align with swaps trading and market structure as explained in Section III.H. Second, the framework would draw upon the CFTC's long and esteemed history as a principles-based regulator to implement a flexible core principles-based approach for SEFs that aligns with the way swaps actually trade. Prescriptive rules, such as those discussed in Section III.H., would be removed. To implement such an approach, the framework would allow SEFs to work with the Commission to achieve the objectives of the core principles within the context of the unique construct and practices of modern swaps markets. In the words of a former CFTC Chairman, "What matters in a principles-based approach is not a focus on means, but rather effectiveness in achieving the desired policy outcomes .... In such a rapidly evolving industry, having the option to rely upon a flexible, principles approach provides a useful tool in carrying out our mandate under the CEA to promote responsible innovation and fair competition."[265]

This approach treats SEFs less like DCM SROs, and more like platforms that operate in a competitive, institutional client market. This approach also considers the episodic liquidity of swaps and the multi-polar structure of the swaps market. This flexible approach would promote swaps trading under CFTC regulation as Congress intended.

---

[264] *See* SEF Rule at 33,480-483. *See also* CFTC Letter No. 13-81, *Time-Limited No-Action Relief from Required Transaction Execution Methods for Transactions that Result from Basis Risk Mitigation Services* (Dec. 23, 2013), *available at* http://www.cftc.gov/ucm/groups/public/@lrlettergeneral/documents/letter/13-81.pdf (allowing basis risk mitigation services under certain conditions).

[265] Reuben Jeffery III, Chairman, Crafting Regulatory Policy to Meet Today's Challenge, Address by Chairman Reuben Jeffery III, Futures Industry Association, 32nd Annual International Futures Industry Conference, Boca Raton, Florida (Mar. 15, 2007), *available at* http://www.cftc.gov/PressRoom/SpeechesTestimony/opajeffery-16.

D. Professionalism

The fourth tenet of this White Paper's alternative framework is to raise standards of professionalism in the swaps market by setting standards of conduct for swaps market personnel. More than any single event, the 2008 financial crisis confirmed the need for greater CCP clearing of swaps and reporting trades to centralized data repositories. The crisis serves less well, however, as a singular justification for the need to regulate swaps trading and execution. AIG did not fail because of flawed market practices or a lack of pre-trade price transparency.[266] Although many market participants were under-collateralized for their swaps inventories, the markets themselves functioned satisfactorily through the crisis.[267] And, while credit default protection against the failure of even the most "too big to fail" bank became very expensive in September 2008, it remained available in the swaps markets, which continued to provide reasonable liquidity despite the broad market fear and panic.[268]

A stronger justification for regulation of swaps trading and execution is presented by the current scandal over pricing of LIBOR[269] and certain foreign exchange benchmarks.[270] In the LIBOR scandal, traders at some dealer banks and allied brokers at some interdealer brokerage firms falsely manipulated quotations of interest rates they

---

[266] AIG held approximately $28 billion of largely unhedged exposure to collateralized debt and mortgage obligations. AIG made a bad investment decision to expose itself to mortgages that went sour. The problem was that AIG made that bad decision, not that AIG paid too much for that bad decision due to pre-trade price opacity. Nor was it likely that any systemic breakdown would have occurred if AIG had been allowed to fail. *See* Wallison 412-416.

[267] Choi and Shachar at 10-17.

[268] *Id.*

[269] *See, e.g.,* Liam Vaughan & Gavin Finch, *Libor Lies Revealed in Rigging of $300 Trillion Benchmark*, Bloomberg, Jan. 28, 2013, *available at* http://www.bloomberg.com/news/2013-01-28/libor-lies-revealed-in-rigging-of-300-trillion-benchmark.html. LIBOR is an average interest rate calculated through submissions of interest rates by major banks in London. LIBOR underpins approximately $350 trillion in derivatives. LIBOR is used as a reference rate in many financial products, including mortgages, student loans, financial derivatives, and other instruments. LIBOR is a common reference rate for interest rate swaps and other derivative instruments traded in U.S. derivatives markets. Any manipulation of LIBOR may constitute an attempt to manipulate U.S. derivatives markets.

[270] *See, e.g.,* Chad Bray, *A Primer on How Currency Manipulation Worked*, DealBook, The New York Times, Nov. 12, 2014, *available at* http://dealbook.nytimes.com/2014/11/12/a-primer-on-how-currency-manipulation-worked/?_r=0; Press Release, *CFTC Orders Five Banks to Pay over $1.4 Billion in Penalties for Attempted Manipulation of Foreign Exchange Benchmark Rates*, CFTC (Nov. 12, 2014), *available at* http://www.cftc.gov/PressRoom/PressReleases/pr7056-14.

were paying or were expecting to pay, to borrow from other major banks.[271] This was done primarily to inflate the bank's creditworthiness and, in many cases, to profit from trading strategies based on movements in LIBOR driven by the inclusion of these false interest rate quotes.[272]

The LIBOR scandal and allegations of similar behavior in setting foreign exchange rates serve as an appropriate basis for regulatory action to enhance professionalism in the swaps markets by ensuring standards of participant conduct. The fraudulent conduct of the traders and brokers implicated in the LIBOR scandal suggests a lack of consistent professionalism and ethical behavior at the trading level. United Kingdom authorities have reorganized their regulatory oversight to focus on failures in appropriate conduct in London financial markets.[273] The new Financial Conduct Authority (FCA) regulates firms under its jurisdiction by proactively setting high conduct standards and exercising supervision and enforcement authority.[274] The FCA has promised "a renewed focus on wholesale conduct" to ensure "trust in the integrity of markets" and prevent "market abuse."[275]

This White Paper proposes like action by the CFTC to increase professionalism by setting standards for participant conduct in regulated swaps trading. It is noteworthy that U.S. individuals who wish to broker or sell equities or debt securities must register

---

[271] *See, e.g.,* In the Matter of: Barclays PLC, Barclays Bank PLC and Barclays Capital Inc., Order Instituting Proceedings Pursuant to Sections 6(c) and 6(d) of the Commodity Exchange Act, as Amended, Making Findings and Imposing Remedial Sanctions, CFTC Docket No. 12-25, *available at* http://www.cftc.gov/ucm/groups/public/@lrenforcementactions/documents/legalpleading/enfbarclaysorder 062712.pdf.

[272] *Id.*

[273] Kim Durniat, *Goodbye FSA, Hello PRA and FCA*, Barnett Waddingham, Apr. 3, 2014, *available at* http://www.barnett-waddingham.co.uk/comment-insight/blog/2013/04/03/goodbye-fsa-hello-pra-and-fca/.

[274] Financial Conduct Authority (FCA), Regulating, http://www.fca.org.uk/about/what/regulating (last accessed Jan. 9, 2015); FCA, Championing, http://www.fca.org.uk/about/what/championing (last accessed Jan. 9, 2015). *See also* Sam Robinson, *The Financial Conduct Authority - Its Role in the New UK Regulatory Framework*, Bloomberg BNA (Aug. 5, 2014), *available at* http://www.bna.com/the-financial-conduct-authority/.

[275] Bank Governance Leadership Network, *A New Era of Conduct Supervision: Consequences, Challenges, and Opportunities*, ViewPoints, Tapestry Networks, Inc., at 2 (Mar. 21, 2014), *available at* http://www.ey.com/Publication/vwLUAssets/EY_-_Navigating_the_new_era_of_conduct_supervision/$FILE/ey-A-new-era-of-conduct-supervision.pdf.

with the SEC and join an SRO.[276] They must also pass the Series 7 exam, which seeks to measure the knowledge, skills and abilities needed to perform the functions of a registered securities representative.[277] Similarly, in U.S. futures markets persons acting as introducing brokers (IBs), futures commission merchants (FCMs), commodity trading advisors (CTAs), commodity pool operators (CPOs) and retail foreign exchange dealers (RFEDs), or an associated person (AP)[278] of such futures professionals, must register with the CFTC and National Futures Association (NFA). Generally, all applicants for NFA membership must pass the Series 3 exam, which seeks to measure futures markets proficiency.[279] Yet, there is currently no examination that one must pass in the U.S. to broker swaps. There is currently no standardized measurement of one's knowledge and qualification to act with discretion in the world's largest and, arguably, most systemically important financial market – swaps.[280]

Rather than implementing highly prescriptive swaps trading rules that seek to limit intermediaries' (*e.g.,* interdealer brokers, FCMs, IBs) discretion through certain ill-suited execution methods,[281] this alternative framework proposes to establish standards

---

[276] *See* SEC, Guide to Broker-Dealer Registration (Apr. 2008), http://www.sec.gov/divisions/marketreg/bdguide.htm#II (last accessed Jan. 9, 2015).
[277] *See* Financial Industry Regulatory Authority (FINRA), General Securities Representative Qualification Examination (Series 7) Content Outline (2014), *available at* http://www.finra.org/web/groups/industry/@ip/@comp/@regis/documents/industry/p124292.pdf.
[278] 17 C.F.R. 1.3(aa).
[279] *See* National Futures Association (NFA), Registration, Who Has to Register, http://www.nfa.futures.org/NFA-registration/index.HTML (last accessed Jan. 9, 2015); NFA, Proficiency Requirements, http://www.nfa.futures.org/NFA-registration/proficiency-requirements.HTML (last accessed Jan. 9, 2015); NFA, Examination Subject Areas National Commodity Futures Exam, *available at* http://www.nfa.futures.org/NFA-registration/study-outlines/SO-Series3.pdf.
[280] The Dodd-Frank Act requires registration of swap dealers (SDs) and major swap participants (MSPs), and directed the Commission to promulgate specific business conduct requirements and "such other standards and requirements as the Commission may determine are appropriate in the public interest, for the protection of investors, or otherwise in furtherance of the purposes of this Act." CEA sections 4s(a), 4s(h) and 4s(h)(3)(D); 7 U.S.C. 6s(a), 6s(h) and 6s(h)(3)(D). Pursuant to this direction the Commission issued business conduct standards for SDs and MSPs in Part 23 of its regulations. Those regulations do not require any sort of proficiency testing, however. Moreover, APs of SDs and MSPs are not required to register under the Dodd-Frank Act or the Commission's regulations. *See* Registration of Swap Dealers and Major Swap Participants, 77 FR 2613 (Jan. 19, 2012).
[281] Apparently, an objection of the CFTC staff for Dutch Auction swap execution is that brokers have discretion in finding price points at which to commence an auction. This same concern regarding discretion is present in the conditions that CFTC staff have outlined for basis risk mitigation services. *See* CFTC Letter No. 13-81, *Time-Limited No-Action Relief from Required Transaction Execution Methods for Transactions that Result from Basis Risk Mitigation Services* (Dec. 23, 2013), *available at* http://www.cftc.gov/ucm/groups/public/@lrlettergeneral/documents/letter/13-81.pdf (see condition 7).

that would enhance the knowledge, professionalism and ethics of personnel in the U.S. swaps markets that exercise discretion in facilitating swaps execution, as well as certain supporting compliance and operations personnel.

As explained in Section I., the episodic liquidity and customized nature of swaps transactions often require intermediaries to arrange trades. Intermediaries' discretion cannot be usurped by machines. Just as today's equity IPO markets retain the presence of competent human professionals to exercise judgment and discretion in trade execution to avoid run-away electronic automated trading dynamics, so do global swaps markets require trained and skilled professionals to foster orderly markets with adequate trading liquidity to meet counterparty demand. This proposal seeks to implement an examination regime for interdealer brokers and other personnel to assure they are up to this important task.[282]

This alternative proposal would focus on raising the knowledge, skills, professionalism, ethics and conduct of key personnel at interdealer brokers, FCMs, IBs, swap dealers and major swap participants, among other entities acting in the swaps market. The proposal would look to established precedents, such as the NFA's Series 3 exam and rules for IBs and other members,[283] as well as the Financial Industry Regulatory Authority's (FINRA) Series 7 exam and rules for broker-dealers,[284] as a guide and modify them to apply to swaps trading and markets (*e.g.,* by creating a licensing exam and rules specifically for swaps).[285] Regulators would work with the

---

[282] Any examination must be designed to reflect the unique nature of the swaps market, such as the absence of retail participation.

[283] *See* NFA, NFA Manual / Rules, Compliance Rules, *available at* https://www.nfa.futures.org/nfamanual/NFAManualTOC.aspx?Section=4.

[284] *See* FINRA, FINRA Rules, *available at* http://finra.complinet.com/en/display/display.html?rbid=2403&element_id=607.

[285] *E.g.,* The Series 7 exam is for individuals who want to enter the securities industry to sell any type of security. The Series 14 exam is designed to assess the competency of compliance officials. The Series 24 exam is designed to assess the competency of entry-level General Securities Principals. The Series 99 exam is designed to assess the competency of certain operations personnel. *See* FINRA, FINRA Administered Qualifications Examinations, *available at* http://www.finra.org/Industry/Compliance/Registration/QualificationsExams/Qualifications/p011096 (providing further details).

industry to understand the testing, qualifications, trading standards and sanctions that should apply to intermediaries and other personnel.[286]

In the preamble to the final SEF rules, the CFTC already acknowledges that a SEF must establish and enforce rules for its employees, and that a SEF's employees have certain obligations under the CFTC's existing regulations.[287] This alternative framework would create a formal process and rules to implement and expand upon the CFTC's preamble language. This approach would bring the swaps market more in line with the regulation of trading intermediaries in other capital markets, such as equities and futures. If done correctly, this approach would provide an exemplary model for the world to follow.

E. Transparency

The last tenet of this White Paper's alternative framework focuses on promoting swaps trading and market liquidity as a prerequisite to increased transparency. It is certainly true that the right measure of pre- and post-trade transparency can benefit market liquidity. Yet, the history of markets has shown that absolute transparency can harm liquidity and trading.[288] The regulatory objective must be to strike the right balance and do so in a progressive manner.[289] Markets as complex as the swaps markets, where adequate liquidity is already a challenge, require care in the imposition of transparency mandates to ensure that this liquidity is not harmed.

As explained in Section III.A., Congress understood the liquidity challenge in the swaps market and thus set two goals for SEFs, to be balanced against each other: (a)

---

[286] To the extent that a person must register as an FCM or IB, Commission and NFA standard of conduct-type rules should be modified to apply to swaps trading.

[287] SEF Rule at 33,506.

[288] There are historical examples of markets that have sought to achieve full market transparency without adequate exemptions. In 1986, the London Stock Exchange (LSE) enacted post-trade reporting rules designed for total transparency with no exceptions for block sizes. What ensued was a sharp drop in trading liquidity as market makers withdrew from the market due to increased trading risk. ISDA/SIFMA Block Trade Study at 8. To bring back trading, the LSE thereafter engaged in a series of amendments to make its block trade rules more flexible and detailed over time. *Id.* at 8-9.

[289] It is worth noting that the trade reporting regime that is often cited positively as a model for swaps trade reporting is the TRACE system for U.S. corporate bonds that was phased in gradually and iteratively over several years.

promoting the trading of swaps on SEFs and (b) promoting pre-trade price transparency in the swaps market.[290] To date, pre-trade price transparency has been greatly emphasized to the detriment of liquidity.[291] SEFs are required to offer an Order Book or an RFQ System to 3 market participants.[292] Other SEF execution methods that do not fit within these narrow rules have been or are in jeopardy of being rejected.[293] Yet, over one year into SEF trading, the Order Book method of execution – the method of execution that is promoted as providing the greatest degree of pre-trade price transparency – has failed to gain traction.[294] Neither SEF goal is being achieved by requiring an Order Book that no one is using. The CFTC's over-engineered and restrictive swaps trading rules have wholly failed to achieve a key objective of meaningful price transparency. It is time to try something different.

A better way to promote price transparency is through a balanced focus on promoting swaps trading and market liquidity as Congress intended. Instead of taking a prescriptive approach to swaps execution that drives away participants, this framework would allow the market to innovate and provide execution through "any means of interstate commerce." That way, participants could choose the execution method that meets their needs based upon a swap's liquidity characteristics, which in turn, promotes trading on SEFs and liquidity. As explained in Section I.D., trading platforms pre-Dodd-Frank Act calibrated their execution methods to the particular liquidity characteristics of the instruments traded and sought to foster the greatest degree of trading liquidity. These execution methodologies, such as hybrid methods, work-up and Dutch Auctions seek to concentrate liquidity by bringing participants together and enabling them to execute orders based on transparent prices. In other words, promoting swaps trading and market liquidity will lead to enhanced price transparency; stifling trading liquidity will degrade it.

---

[290] CEA section 5h(e); 7 U.S.C. 5h(e).
[291] *See, e.g.,* Section III.A.
[292] *Id.*
[293] *Id.* and Section IV.E.
[294] *See* Madigan, Anonymity ("The volume so far has been mostly RFQ ... Clients can use the Clobs ... somewhere north of 95% of our client flows are going through our RFQ system," says Lee Olesky, chief executive of Tradeweb in New York.). *See also* Lynn Strongin Dodds, *SEFs: A Slow Start So Far,* DerivSource, Nov. 17, 2014, *available at* http://derivsource.com/articles/sefs-slow-start-so-far.

The pro-reform proposals set forth in this White Paper are a package. They stand together as a comprehensive whole. It would serve little purpose to reassert the broad reach of SEF registration without easing the rigid inflexibility of the CFTC's swap transaction rules. It would make little sense to seek to improve standards of participant conduct without removing the unwarranted restraints on their professional discretion. It would be pointless to seek greater market transparency while continuing to thwart market liquidity. These proposals work together to achieve the aims of Title VII of the Dodd-Frank Act to improve the safety and soundness of the U.S. swaps market. They should not be adopted on a piecemeal basis.

VI. CONCLUSION: Return to Congressional Intent

In September 2014, the largest U.S.-listed IPO of all time occurred on the NYSE when Alibaba, the Chinese e-commerce giant, raised over $25 billion.[295] In fact, the third quarter of 2014 was great for U.S. IPOs with over $40 billion raised as compared with $8.6 billion raised in Europe and $14.3 billion in Asia.[296] During the quarter, U.S. markets overall accounted for 52 percent of cross-border IPO activity.[297] The U.S. is ranked as the top country for new equity fundraisings for the fourth straight year.[298]

Why did Alibaba choose New York to offer its shares rather than major exchanges in Asia and Europe? Certainly, the depth of U.S. equity liquidity necessary for a blockbuster offering drew in Alibaba. Yet, companies big and small from around the world flock to the U.S. IPO market. Is it only trading liquidity, or does it also have to do with the balance of favorable market characteristics and a proven and well-respected U.S. regulatory framework?

According to the head of equity capital markets at Nomura, "[f]lexibility around governance provisions and the reputation for US capital markets as a whole" make the U.S. a premier place to list.[299] Flexibility in corporate governance provisions was important to Alibaba.[300] U.S. listing rules permitted Alibaba's unique board structure, which the Hong Kong Stock Exchange prohibited.[301] Yet, no one can assert that the flexibility afforded Alibaba makes the U.S. a lax and lenient jurisdiction in which to list shares. The SEC's public company disclosure regime and registration process is likely the world's most rigorous. However, it is globally recognized that the U.S. IPO market

---

[295] Includes the overallotment exercise.

[296] Leslie Picker, Ruth David and Fox Hu, *IPO Markets Don't Need Alibaba for Best Quarter Since 2010*, Bloomberg, Sep. 30, 2014, *available at* http://www.bloomberg.com/news/2014-09-30/ipo-markets-don-t-need-alibaba-for-best-third-quarter-since-2010.html.

[297] *Id.*

[298] Jackie Kelley, *US Leads The World in 2014 IPOs*, Forbes, Dec. 23, 2014, *available at* http://www.forbes.com/sites/ey/2014/12/23/us-leads-the-world-in-2014-ipos/; Eric Platt and Josh Noble, *New York Widens Global Lead for IPOs*, Financial Times, Sep. 29, 2014 (Platt & Noble), *available at* http://www.ft.com/intl/cms/s/0/821ee226-45c1-11e4-9b71-00144feabdc0.html?siteedition=intl#axzz3IsqLvLYD.

[299] Platt & Noble.

[300] *Id.*

[301] *Id.*

has a highly optimal balance of robust regulation, fulsome corporate disclosure, human discretion and flexible corporate compliance as compared with its peer marketplaces. As a result, the world and its capital seek out the U.S. IPO market, bringing along jobs and economic growth.

As compared with the recently resurgent global interest in the U.S. IPO market, however, the world's response to the CFTC's newly implemented swaps trading regulations has been a stark "No, thank you." As discussed in Section IV.A., the world is voting with its trading book to transact in other markets whenever possible. Non-U.S. person market participants are curtailing transactions with U.S. counterparties to avoid the CFTC's ill-designed and highly prescriptive U.S. swaps trading rules.

In his best-selling book, *The Great Degeneration: How Institutions Decay and Economies Die*, Niall Ferguson describes contemporary financial market regulation that well-characterizes the CFTC's swaps trading rules:

> Today …the balance of opinion favours complexity over simplicity; rules over discretion; codes of compliance over individual and corporate responsibility. I believe this approach is based on a flawed understanding of how financial markets work. It puts me in mind of the great Viennese satirist Karl Kraus' famous quip about psychoanalysis; that it was the disease of which it pretended to be the cure. I believe excessively complex regulation is the disease of which it pretends to be the cure.[302]

This paper has attempted to explain why the world has shunned the CFTC's swaps trading regime. The fundamental problem is that the CFTC's regime is over-engineered and mismatched to the distinct liquidity, trading and market structure characteristics of the global swaps markets. In crafting a swaps trading regulatory framework disproportionately modeled after the U.S. futures market, and imposing it through complicated and highly prescriptive rules in contravention of congressional intent, the CFTC is driving trading liquidity away from U.S. markets. The current regime is causing global swaps trading to fragment into U.S. person markets and non-U.S. person markets, exacerbating the inherent challenge of swaps trading – adequate

---

[302] Niall Ferguson, The Great Degeneration: How Institutions Decay and Economies Die 58-59 (Penguin Press 2013).

liquidity. The result will be higher costs and burdens for U.S. risk hedging and slower American economic growth and job creation. Undoubtedly, these added costs will be borne harder on Main Street than on Wall Street.

This paper proposes an alternative, pro-reform agenda. It advocates for a comprehensive, cohesive and flexible alternative swaps trading framework that aligns with swaps market dynamics and is true to congressional intent. The framework is built upon five broad tenets: comprehensiveness, cohesiveness, flexibility, professionalism and transparency. This framework should yield enormous benefits. It would promote healthy global markets by regulating swaps trading in a manner well matched to the underlying market dynamics. It may undo much of the global fragmentation in swaps trading and the resulting increased systemic risk by drawing the global trading community to the CFTC's swaps regime, rather than rejecting it. The framework would relieve much of the developing domestic market fragmentation and promote trading liquidity – an inherent challenge in the swaps market. It would help reduce the enormous legal and compliance costs of registering and operating a CFTC-registered SEF. This framework would encourage technological innovation to better serve market participants and preserve the jobs of U.S.-based support personnel. It would free up CFTC resources and save taxpayer money at a time of federal budget deficits. It would provide the CFTC with another opportunity to coordinate its rules with other jurisdictions that are implementing their own swaps trading rules. It may even reverse the increasing fragility of U.S. swaps markets by allowing their more organic development and growth for the greater benefit of U.S. economic health and prosperity. Most critically, it would fully accord with Title VII of the Dodd-Frank Act.

In releasing this White Paper, I am conscious that it invariably will be drawn into the preconceived storyline that seems to frame all contemporary discussions of the 2008 financial crisis and the Dodd-Frank Act. Depending on one's political persuasion, that set narrative generally features, on one side, either valiant market reformers striving to prevent another financial crisis or faceless bureaucrats stifling legitimate business activity, while on the other side are feckless toadies for Wall Street working to "roll back" regulatory reform or brave souls speaking "truth to power" to the same faceless bureaucrats.

This false narrative is especially challenging for me as an unwavering supporter of the core swaps reforms of Title VII of the Dodd-Frank Act. Because I come at these reforms from the real world of commerce, I am not satisfied with loudly trumpeted agency rules that work only on paper as academic exercises. Effective regulation must perform efficiently in the reality of everyday global markets or it will produce useless, counterproductive or even harmful consequences.

Fortunately, some of the Dodd-Frank rules put in place by the CFTC have worked well out of the box. Others need to be fine-tuned. Some need to be replaced altogether. The false narrative that all Dodd-Frank rules were perfect at conception and are now sacrosanct is just that – false.[303] The perpetuation of this narrative makes it harder to achieve the purposes that the law seeks to advance: financial market reform and systemic risk reduction. My hope is that coverage of this White Paper and its pro-reform proposals, perhaps fueled by increasing market awareness of the identified regulatory flaws, will reflect less partisan reporting. That will lower the emotional thermostat as the CFTC begins the necessary process of rule repair and replacement.

I urge my fellow Commissioners and CFTC staff to revisit our agency's fundamentally flawed swaps trading rules and replace them with a more coherent framework that follows congressional intent and aligns with the natural commercial workings of the swaps market. Such a framework will achieve Congress's express goals of promoting swaps trading and market transparency in a well-conceived regulatory framework without exacerbating systemic risk and market fragility.

Derivatives are vital to the U.S. economy. Used properly, they enable American companies and the banks from which they borrow to manage changing commodity and energy prices, fluctuating currency and interest rates and credit default exposure. They

---

[303] The recent TRIA legislation that amended the Dodd-Frank Act to exempt non-financial firms, such as farmers and manufacturers, from having to post collateral in derivatives transactions was passed with overwhelmingly bipartisan political support. *See generally,* Zachary Warmbrodt, *Democrats' Quandary: Which Dodd-Frank Changes Weaken the Law?*, POLITICOPro, Jan. 8, 2015.

allow state and local governments to manage their obligations and pension funds to support healthy retirements. They allow agricultural producers to hedge their prices and costs of production so that Americans enjoy plenty of food on grocery shelves. They allow Americans to rely on enough electricity to run their homes and gasoline to fuel their cars. The health and efficiency of the derivatives markets have a direct impact on the price and availability of the food we eat, the warmth of our homes and the energy needed to power our factories.

The stated purpose of the Dodd-Frank Act was to reform "Wall Street." That task must be completed in a way that does not burden "Main Street" by adding new compliance costs onto our farmers, power utilities and manufacturers. It is the job of market regulators like the CFTC to promote U.S. markets with smart regulations rather than impede them with unwarranted costs and over-engineered complexity. U.S. financial markets have long been the most fair, transparent, efficient and innovative in the world. We must keep them so. Our goal in this new era must be the health of markets and the regeneration of the spirit of American enterprise – a spirit that rekindles some of our lost prosperity and puts everyday people back to work.

A smarter and more flexible swaps regulatory framework would enable the U.S. to take the global lead in smart regulation of swaps trading, just as it does with IPOs. It would allow American businesses to more efficiently hedge commercial risks, promoting economic growth. Such a framework would also stimulate the American jobs market. A smarter swaps regulatory regime would return to the express letter and language of Title VII of the Dodd-Frank Act. It would eschew the artificial slicing and dicing of U.S. trading liquidity and unwarranted restrictions on means of execution that are unsupported by the law. A smarter swaps regulatory framework should be built upon the five tenets discussed herein: comprehensiveness, cohesiveness, flexibility, professionalism and transparency. For decades the CFTC has been a competent and effective regulator of U.S. exchange-traded derivatives. The opportunity is at hand to continue that excellence in regulating swaps markets. It is time to seize that opportunity.

About the Author

J. Christopher Giancarlo was nominated by President Obama on August 1, 2013, and was sworn in as a Commissioner of the U.S. Commodity Futures Trading Commission on June 16, 2014 for a term expiring in April 2019.

Commissioner Giancarlo practiced corporate and securities law for 16 years in New York and London. Thereafter, he served for over a dozen years as a senior executive of a publicly-traded operator and provider of swaps trading platforms and trading software and technology used worldwide. Commissioner Giancarlo helped that firm launch and develop its operations in 16 global financial centers.

Commissioner Giancarlo was also a founding Co-Editor-in-Chief of eSecurities, Trading and Regulation on the Internet (Leader Publications). In addition, Commissioner Giancarlo has testified three times before Congress regarding the implementation of the Dodd-Frank Act, and has written and spoken extensively on public policy, legal and other matters involving technology and the financial markets.

Commissioner Giancarlo believes that vibrant, open and competitive markets are an essential element to a strong U.S. economy. He has been a consistent advocate for practical and effective implementation of the following three pillars of Title VII of the Dodd-Frank Act: enhanced swaps transparency, regulated swaps execution and central counterparty clearing. His support for these reforms is based simply on practical experience. Commissioner Giancarlo believes that balanced and well-drafted regulatory oversight should go hand-in-hand with open and competitive markets, economic growth, and American job creation.